Night Stalker Richard Ramirez

The Horrifying True Crime Story of the

Infamous Serial Killer

By

James Richmond

Table of Contents

Intro

August 31, 1985. The heat was sweltering. That whole summer had been a restless surge of feverish temperatures. There was no breeze to provide relief, and that was all the citizens of California wanted—relief from this nightmare. The unforgiving sun broke the line of the horizon and crested over the mass of shining skyscrapers. Fear in the city of Los Angeles was omnipresent, looming around every corner in the sickening wave of warmth.

At exactly 7:25 a.m. a Greyhound bus pulled into the parking lot, arriving from Phoenix, Arizona. The passengers disembarked one by one after the long ride, and unknown to the rest, among them was one of America's most dangerous serial killers.

Tall, with a lithe, thin frame, he stepped off the bus dressed in all black. Sleep from the journey was heavy in his tired, red eyes. A black backpack draped over his shoulder. He glanced around lazily, making his way into the bus terminal. His Walkman blasted heavy metal in his ear, and his thick, curly hair bounced with each step. Inside the terminal, the air was cool.

Richard Ramirez was finally home.

He hadn't slept well on the ride, nor had he eaten. He was thirsty as well. After stopping to use the restroom, it was time for Richard to grab a bite to eat. No one took notice of him as he moved about the station.

But fifteen men waited. They thought Richard would be leaving L.A. None dared think he'd be arriving back to where a massive search had begun twelve hours prior. They studied the departing buses, completely unaware that the man they hunted was back in the city. Over the last six months, more than twenty California homes had fallen victim to Richard's hands. Some were murdered, others raped, molested, or tortured. Every news outlet and newspaper in the area had Richard Ramirez's face plastered on the front.

But no one bothered him as he left the bus station and passed several security guards.

Underneath the blazing sun, the sweat immediately collected along Richard's brow. He picked up a nickel bag of pot and headed to a liquor store on South Town Avenue. He purchased a beverage as well as a sweet pastry to snack on as he started his day. A few people gave him passing glances, but Richard was not one to be bothered by them. His rotting teeth and dark aesthetic tended to catch an eyebrow raise every now and then.

Standing at the cash register, he removed three one-dollar bills from his wallet, passed it to the cashier, and waited for his change. As the glances began to turn more into stares, he plucked the headphones of his Walkman from his ears. Out of the corner of his eye, he noticed several elderly Mexican women. They stood together in the back of the store, their gaze transfixed on him. Richard's heartbeat quickened. Their gaze immediately broke when he caught them. Whispers grew between them.

His paranoia was probably nothing more than the effect of the cocaine he'd shot up his arm earlier in the bus station bathroom. He'd just refilled his stash while visiting family in Arizona.

He looked away, and this time his eyes fell to the stack of *La Opinion* newspapers on either side of the register. Beads of sweat gathered on his skin. His focus flickered back down to the image in the newspaper. Dark, hollow eyes stared hauntingly back at his own. At first, the portrait that covered the front page meant nothing. It took him a second before the realization came crashing down. The cat-like eyes, high cheekbones, and scruffy dark hair all belonged to a face he knew well.

His own.

Richard's heart leaped into his throat. Panic rolled through him as adrenaline doused his system. His image was on the front page of every newspaper. The customers watched him with wide eyes, and now even as he looked back, none looked away.

Behind him, he heard one of the elderly women speak. Her finger outstretched, pointing.

"El Matador," she said.

The Killer.

After a brutal and deadly year, California's Night Stalker finally had a face.

The summer of 1985 was a time of extreme horror for Los Angeles as the Night Stalker prowled along the suburban streets, looking for any random home to slink into and unfurl unspeakable horrors upon. It was one of the hottest summers on record, but none dared open their windows to let in the cool night air. Paralyzed by fear and the sweltering heat, the citizens of L.A. were no longer safe in their neighborhoods.

Over the course of two years, Richard Ramirez terrorized the community like an invisible shadow. The tortured man believed Satan watched over him like a guardian demon, as some sort of protector who encouraged these savage acts against the community. At the age of twenty-nine, he was convicted of thirteen murders, five attempted murders, eleven sexual assaults, and fourteen burglaries.

Born the youngest of five children to two hard-working immigrants, the Ramirez family lived a hard life. A series of accidents and dangerous influences turned the once kind, wide-eyed boy into what is now considered one of America's most evil and vile men. He rebelled against his parents, took myriad drugs, and found himself fantasizing more and more about bondage and rape. Whether or not he was born to become a serial killer there is no way of knowing, but the experiences Richard lived through helped groom him into the monster he became. He was taught to steal, and it was ingrained in him by his cousin. At a young age, Richard's view of the world was warped. He turned from the Catholic influence of his parents and accepted Satan with open arms. He believed the Devil was the only being who truly accepted him.

With the strength of Satan, Ramirez murdered, raped, and mutilated his way through Southern California. He had no type, no preferred victim. All Richard needed was for his prey to simply be at home the moment he arrived at their doorstep or window. His goal was solely based on instilling violence and fear. Murder and rape were all he required. His victims ranged in race, age, and gender. The police were at a loss, and for a while, believed it was impossible these murders were done by the same person.

As Richard put it, "I murder simply because I love it."

His methods and weapons switched depending on what he could find at the time or what would be the most horrifying. He stole and took as he pleased, believing he deserved whatever he wanted. Dreams of a grand life filled his head, full of slaves to serve him.

Ramirez wanted to be seen as a supernatural force, a weapon of hell itself, but to most, he is looked at as nothing more than a vile monster who preyed upon the weak to fulfill his sick sexual fantasies. He was a serial killer unlike any other, and until 1984, one so gruesome America had never seen anything like him.

Deputy District Attorney Philip Halpin said Richard Ramirez's murderous acts were so vile and dark, he "probably rewrote the book on serial murders."

Yet through his trials, hordes of women poured into and around the courthouse to catch a glimpse of Satan's bad boy. He amassed a following and stole the media spotlight. Fan mail from across the world flooded to Richard's jail cell.

Richard Ramirez, who started off as nothing more than a lowlife scum, became such a horrible monster that he left a legacy behind him. For many, Ramirez was living proof of the Devil. To those people, he was evidence that a Satanic force implemented itself on Earth, forcing people to commit atrocious crimes. An era of panic emerged, and Richard Ramirez was a catalyst for it. His outspoken devotion and sinister acts shaped the way Americans live to this day. Richard had done his job in spreading misery and the palpable fear that the Devil is indeed real.

A Hopeful Start

February 16, 1927. In Camargo, Mexico, Julian Tapia Ramirez's humble beginnings started on a poor farm. The farm's landscape was hot, brutal, and surrounded by mountains. As the second-oldest of eight and the firstborn son, life for Julian was challenging. His days were spent toiling on the family's farm. At twelve, his mother passed away, leaving him in the complete care of his father, José Ramirez, and grandfather. Both were serious, hard men who matched the brutal, unwavering lands surrounding their farm. If any of his eight children misbehaved, José beat them. Physical punishment was common at the time in rural Mexico, but José's temper was vile. It was explosive, and José lost it often, usually on his oldest son. Out of all eight children, Julian received the wrath of his father and grandfather the most. It wasn't uncommon for him to be tied to a tree while his father or grandfather used a thick rope to whip him. The abuse and fear turned Julian quiet and withdrawn. He learned to silently wait through the bouts of rage that overtook José and his grandfather. He did not speak nor fight back.

After first grade, Julian was pulled out of school. Hours of his precious childhood were spent underneath the blazing sun. Without a complaint, he slaved away on his father's farm. Finally, at the age of fourteen, he had gone through enough. Julian stood up against his father. He threw José's leather belt on the ground and demanded to never be beaten again. His behavior was a serious act of defiance, but his father respected his demands. He never hit the boy again.

Despite all of the punishment, Julian was an overall good son. He never cursed or smoked, and only on occasion would have a drink. Every Sunday, he attended church with his family and was a strong Christian, who feared the power of the Devil.

It was also in his fourteenth year when he met Mercedes Muñoz, who had moved from Rocky Ford, Colorado to Camargo, Mexico during World War II. Her grandmother made the move out of fear that one of her sons would be drafted in the war. New to the city, Mercedes befriended one of Julian's sisters. It was only a matter of time until the two officially met. Though it took five years for a real romance to blossom, at nineteen years old, the two began to see one another. They went on dates, sometimes on walks under the cool night sky in the city's only park or to the cinema.

The small community of Camargo offered little work. The Muñoz family decided to move to Juarez, a bordering town of El Paso, in August 1947. And since the Muñoz's children were born in America and therefore natural citizens, they easily found work and traveled between the borders. Mercedes secured a job in El Paso as a housekeeper, though it came with a cost. Her love affair with the handsome, dark-eyed Julian would have to be put on hold or potentially ended.

Julian had been drafted but was dismissed after contracting scarlet fever. His hardened, muscular form weakened due to the disease. Upon returning home, his sister helped nurse him back to health. He wrote to Mercedes. Being in Camargo without her was not the same. Life without one another was empty, and neither found a love as they had with each other. Julian proposed to her in a letter. Even though Mercedes's family thought he was far too poor for her, she agreed to the proposal. She rarely disobeyed her mother, but she truly loved Julian. He was the only man for her, and together they would make their dreams come true.

Julian's father and grandfather were not very fond of the Muñozes in turn. They found Mercedes's family to be far too pompous and stuck up. But together, she and Julian left. Nothing was going to keep them apart any longer. He arrived in Juarez on August 3, 1948, with all his possessions packed into a single cardboard suitcase, and six days later the two were married before a few friends in the Presidency Building. No family attended. All they had was their love and commitment to one another.

There was no honeymoon, only the plan to have a large family with lots of children. They wanted to give their children the life neither of them had been given. Unlike what he grew up experiencing, Julian vowed to never beat his own children.

Being a border state, Juarez is extremely dangerous. Drugs, prostitution, and crime are rampant through the dirt streets. Juarez has a massive population composed of slums stacked on top of one another and factories spewing gas and chemicals through the air. Massive mansions are highly guarded with fences, sitting on high and ruling over the squalor. Mercedes desperately wanted to move. As an American citizen, she continued working in El Paso, but she wanted to raise her children there as well and give them the opportunity to be Americans. Julian was content staying in Mexico, but he could see how badly his young wife needed the change. So, they rented a small apartment in Texas.

Isolated by hard lands, El Paso is America's largest border city, with a population close to one million. Health is an issue there, with disease rates far above the national average. Crime happens often, and drug smuggling over the border runs rampant. The mountain range that stretches through the town is a monstrous divider between the economic classes. The affluent neighborhoods sit on the west, the blue-collar on the east. Poverty is common to the south of the mountains as well. But for Julian and Mercedes, it was their home now, and a steep upgrade from Juarez. They were proud, and seven months later, Mercedes became pregnant.

But two hundred miles away in Los Alamos, New Mexico, the U.S. government was conducting nuclear tests. Though the detonations were far, if the winds blew just right, nuclear fallout made its way over and settled in the lands and the water. During the early part of the 1950s, the rate of birth defects soared, but the government kept the link to the nuclear fallout quiet.

Mercedes and Julian's firstborn son was named Ruben. The pregnancy went well, but Ruben was born with golf-sized lumps on

12

the back of his neck and all over his head. The child was very sick. They called their priest to read his last rites, and together they prayed over their son as he lay in the incubator. Finally, after several days passed, Ruben's health stabilized. The lumps over his body disappeared and though he cried often, he was considered healthy. For the Ramirezes, this was an act of God, answering their hard-fought prayers.

Julian cared for his child. He held his firstborn son, taking long walks through El Paso. The boy's future was valuable. Ruben would have the life Mercedes and Julian had sacrificed everything for. To make that possible, it was important to the young couple that Ruben learn English, unlike his parents.

Two months after Ruben's birth, Mercedes became pregnant once more. This time it was a healthy baby boy named Joseph, after her favorite brother. Julian was over the moon. Two sons in a row was a good omen. He was a very lucky man. He bought cigars to pass around the town and celebrate. Every day he hurried home after work so he could spend time with his two boys.

But Joseph cried often, and each time it felt louder and longer than the previous outburst. Julian walked with him, holding him for hours. Time after time, Julian and Mercedes were told their son was healthy. Joseph was a year old when his parents finally received answers at a clinic—their son was diagnosed with Collier's disease, which causes the bones to curve as they grow. This was potentially the result of poisoning from the nuclear fallout.

The strain of having a severely handicapped son hit the young family hard. They paid for numerous surgeries. The first one came when Joseph was seventeen months old, and while the surgeries helped at first, the condition only worsened over time. Julian and Mercedes were proud, refusing to ask for help. They drove themselves to work harder. News of other birth deformities in the area began to circulate around. Other families were suffering the same terrible fate as the Ramirezes.

With his strong, muscular build Julian secured a job working on a construction site in El Paso. He handled the job well and his employers were pleased, although Julian still lacked the proper papers to work in America.

But in 1952, three immigration officers arrived on the site. They demanded to see Julian's papers. Through the aid of another worker's translation, Julian had to explain his papers had yet to be

14

granted. He tried to tell them his wife was an American citizen, but it didn't matter. Julian was to be deported immediately. They followed him to the small apartment where Mercedes and their two children were living. Despite the protests of the landlord, who fought for his tenant, Julian and his small family were forced to pack up their belongings and were loaded into a truck. Rain fell from the sky as they crossed the Mexican border only to be dumped along with their meager belongings on the side of the road.

Mercedes, with her two sons, returned to her grandmother's house. With the help of her brothers, the young family moved their possessions. Stuck in a desperate situation, Julian expressed to a friend his dire need for work. As luck would have it, he was hired that day as a police officer in Juarez. With his knowledge of guns from his time in the military, he was tasked with training the new officers on how to shoot. But even with his respectable job as a policeman, Mercedes worried for her husband's safety. Juarez was a dangerous city, especially for police who got in the way of elite criminals by being too good at their job.

With the birth of their third son, Robert, Mercedes pushed Julian to continue with his American citizen application.

Finally, it was approved.

During the spring of 1954, the Ramirezes' small troop moved back into El Paso. The hope for their three children to move ahead in life would be possible once again.

Julian landed a job on the Santa Fe railroad. It was hard, laboring work, but his physical strength only grew. The wage was good, though it took him away from his children and family for days at a time. Mercedes had also secured a job at the Tony Lama boot factory. It paid more than housekeeping, and she managed to find women to help watch her three boys while she worked. At Tony Lama, she spent her days mixing pigments for paint then treating the boots with different chemicals. These were toxic—benzene, toluene, and xylene—and required ventilation and a face mask, but Mercedes didn't have either of those. She stood for seven hours a day, five days a week without a fan or window to lessen the toxins' toll. At times, Mercedes was overcome with dizzying fainting spells.

After six months of working at Tony Lama, Mercedes became pregnant with their fourth child. This time it was a girl, who they named Ruth. For Julian and Mercedes, this was wonderful news. Their daughter was healthy and would have three older brothers to

16

protect her. Mercedes finally would have the girl she'd always dreamed of. They continued to put their faith in God, and with four children in five years, they truly felt blessed. Perhaps all their hard work and suffering would pay off. Their conviction would be rewarded.

Julian's sister moved to El Paso with her son Miguel. The family nicknamed him Mike. The sister took a job alongside Mercedes at Tony Lama. They both noticed irritability and a hard change in mood when away from the factory for too long, and grew to believe they'd developed an addiction to the fumes and toxins.

It wasn't long before the Ramirez boys began to attend school. Joseph and Ruben started learning English, and Julian couldn't have been more proud. The other students picked on poor Joseph, though, who learned to walk with special shoes. He handled the comments and jeers of the other students well, but the Ramirez temper had been passed along to the boys. Mercedes took note that all of her children had that same rage as their father. Julian didn't anger often, but when he did, it was violent and extreme. Even young Ruth described her own anger later in life: "I'd just black out when I got mad. I couldn't control the anger. There would just, like, be an explosion inside of me, and I'd go off."

Mercedes became pregnant with their fifth child. It was the most difficult of her pregnancies. She never stopped her work at Tony Lama. The fainting spells became more frequent. She was forced to stop, sit down, and hope the intense bouts of nausea would pass. Sharp cramps and constant fatigue riddled her body. It had been four years since their last child; she and Julian had not planned on having any more. Mercedes went to a specialist who informed her that the chemicals and toxins from her workplace had caused her body to try to reject the pregnancy. She had to receive multiple injections to keep the fetus, and quit her job at Tony Lama at five months into the pregnancy.

Baby of the Family

On February 29, 1960, at 2:07 a.m., Julian loaded up his four children and brought them to the hospital. That winter night in El Paso, they met the youngest of the family born. They named him Ricardo Leyva Muñoz Ramírez. This was especially exciting for Ruth. She fell in love with Richard the moment she laid eyes on him at the hospital. The big-eyed, cooing baby was going to be her real-life doll, and she would be able to play with and care for him.

Over the following years, Joseph continued with the surgeries for his legs to be fixed. He was the mildest of the children, unlike Ruben, who was quick to anger. Ruben and Ruth fought the most, hitting and shouting at one another. They'd bicker often, breaking into squabbles. Robert would get into the fight as well, and if it weren't for Joseph and later Richard, the older boys would have hit Ruth more.

Ruben began to struggle in school. The teachers told the Ramirez parents that their son was displaying behavioral issues. At first, Julian thought it was the other students causing problems for his son, but he quickly came to realize that Ruben was a bit of a rebel.

When the bad report cards started coming home, Julian would beat his son with a garden hose. He wanted to teach his son that there would be consequences if Ruben didn't start making any changes. Their parents came to America for the children to have a better life. Julian worked too hard to have them slack off.

Even with these little episodes, Julian still did what he could to keep his rage from being directed at his children. But they saw it. The first time was in 1963, when Julian struggled with fixing the filter on his car's engine. In frustration and fury, he slammed his head against the house, over and over, until lines of red blood dripped down his face.

But none of Julian's punishments deterred Ruben's disobedience. Instead, he took classes geared for challenged students, because he simply didn't care about achieving. Both Robert, who struggled with a low IQ, and Joseph, who fell behind due to being in the hospital so often, were set back in their studies. This only caused Julian to direct more anger toward Ruben. He had no excuse, unlike his younger brothers.

Richard continued to be doted upon by his older sister, who spoke to him in both Spanish and English. He was a happy baby, hardly fussy. He ate well and had a love for music on the radio. Richard would dance along to it. Even before he was one, he'd move his head and feet along to whatever beat played.

With seven family members under one roof now, the Ramirezes knew it was time to find a bigger place to live. After working and scraping by for eleven years, they managed to purchase a house on Ledo Street. It was a welcoming residential area with single-family homes. Tall trees grew along the streets. It was well-kept and perfect for the Ramirez family. They ended up in the middle of the block with a white, one-story, tract-stucco home. It had three bedrooms, a sizable kitchen, and a backyard. Lace curtains were hung on the windows and a portrait of Jesus giving a blessing tacked on the wall. Every Sunday the family attended mass at El Calvario Catholic Church.

Mercedes continued work at Tony Lama. She found a kind woman named Socorro to stay and watch her children while she spent hours toiling in the harsh factory. With Julian laboring away for days on the railroad, Mercedes needed the help. Little could be done to keep Ruben out of trouble. Even with the new move to a nice neighborhood, his wild antics continued. He found himself among a mischievous group of friends, who spent their time committing petty theft. When Socorro wasn't around and his parents were at work, Ruben would have his friends over, and together they would huff glue. Ruth caught him once, and in response, Ruben threatened to beat his little sister. Out of fear, she didn't tell her parents. Their nanny, Socorro, had little say over what the older boys did, not that they listened much anyway. Ruben ran wild. And with Mercedes and Julian gone most of the time, as long as their parents didn't know, there weren't any issues.

That is, until one day when little Richard asked Socorro to play the radio. He still loved nothing more than listening to music. She promptly told him no. Richard decided then he'd just have to turn the radio on himself. While Socorro remained in a separate room to finish watching her soap opera, he ventured to his parents' bedroom, where a radio sat atop a tall wooden dresser. He climbed up the open drawers, making his way, but upon reaching the third level, his small weight threw the heavy piece of furniture off balance. It came crashing down atop Richard. The two-year-old was knocked unconscious. A deep wound opened on his forehead, where bright red blood ran out profusely.

The noise drew Socorro to the bedroom. The horror of it all drove the nanny into an immediate panic. She lifted the dresser off to find the wounded toddler and pressed a towel to his head, stopping the blood. She phoned Mercedes at work. Dread filled the mother. She raced home, not wasting a second.

At the hospital, Richard received thirty stitches. He remained unconscious for a total of fifteen minutes. The accident left two-year-old Richard with a concussion.

Julian was furious. He exploded upon receiving the news. They knew their young one was hyperactive and never sat still. He needed constant attention. Socorro was clearly not doing her job. Without hesitation, they fired her.

The hard, laborious work of the railroad was taking its toll on Julian. His easy-going personality was disappearing. As time passed, his temper only seemed to grow more serious and quiet, much like his father's.

But his anger truly unleashed when the police call came in one night. Julian was home that evening when the phone rang. Ruben and his cousin Miguel had been caught driving around in a stolen vehicle, sniffing glue. A rage not seen by the family before overcame Julian as he picked up his son from the police station. Whether Ruben had stolen the car or not didn't matter. The arrest was enough to ruin the honest Ramirez name.

Julian slapped Ruben, cursing his son at the police station, but the real punishment occurred when they returned home. All the young children watched, including Richard, as their father laid into Ruben. They ran and hid as they heard the merciless blows reign down on their brother. Ruben cried and hollered in pain. Mercedes prayed, asking for whatever caused her son to pursue such horrid activities to come to an end. Even though Julian had vowed to never lay a hand on his children the way his father and grandfather had done to him, the criminal activities of his son had gone too far. Ruben was covered in bruises after the incident, and Julian made him swear he'd stop hanging around these friends.

But Ruben's promise meant nothing, and as soon as Julian left to return to work, Ruben continued to do as he pleased. His main priorities were getting high and stealing. His rebel attitude only worsened with time, setting off his father's anger.

A second arrest came after Ruben was caught breaking and entering. Once again, Julian inflicted his rage in a series of horrible

24

blows. The children hid in the house as he brought his son home from the police station a second time. He beat him over and over until Mercedes intervened. She supported her husband in punishing their children, but it had gone too far this time.

Julian's rage was now ever-present in the house, looming like a shadow, ready at any moment. The years of back-breaking work on the railroad had made Julian a true force of sheer physical power. But still, Robert followed in his brother's footsteps. And when the two were caught committing crimes and getting in fights with other neighborhood children, Julian's power and rage came through.

During one episode of Julian's rage, he failed to fix the kitchen sink. Joseph, who for the most part stayed out of trouble, stood beside his father, helping him. But Julian began to struggle with fitting the drain pipe in the wall connection. He lost what little patience he had. Curses began to fall from his lips. Joseph sensed the anger stirring like a grizzly bear rising from hibernation. He knew the storm was fast approaching, but running off might anger Julian more. The curses about the sink turned into angry shouts and yells heard throughout the whole house. Everyone knew what was coming. Julian reached for his hammer. The rage inside of him unfurled. He slammed the tool against his head until ribbons of red blood ran down his face. Young Richard saw the blood, heard his father as he took out his rage upon himself.

He'd later describe the fear and feelings that came with his father's outbursts. "I'd seen him beat Ruben and Robert, and I'd seen him lose his temper over the television not working right when he wanted it to. They say it's worse to see someone you love getting tortured or hurt than being tortured or hurt yourself. I don't know if that's true or not, but I was real frightened of my father. When he lost it, I ran and hid, scared shit."

The older brothers made sure to pick on the younger sister. There were five children under one roof, and the antics never fell short. Ruth became good at laughing off the pranks, but Richard wouldn't have any of it if it went too far. He was extremely protective of his sister, and if the other three took it to an extreme, Richard saw red and jumped in the middle to protect her. The Ramirez temper had not skipped the youngest of the brood.

He was a restless child with a wild imagination, playing on his own frequently. One of his favorite games was "Cowboys and Indians," and he'd run around often in the backyard by himself. He did all the parts, acting out the whole story that he created in his mind. Richard aimed his toy gun, shooting at the air, then quickly ran to where he'd shot to fall down, slain by his own hand. The neighbors found this behavior odd, but Mercedes wasn't worried. She was happy her son entertained himself.

When Richard was five years old, his brother Robert brought him along to fetch Ruth one evening. She was at the park near the home, playing. When Richard saw his big sister on a swing, excitement overwhelmed him and he ran to her as fast as he could. Ruth didn't have time to stop. Her swing slammed right into the young Richard's head, giving him a deep gash. He hit the ground hard and was knocked out cold once more. Robert scooped his bloody, unconscious brother in his arms, and they raced home. Upon seeing her son, Mercedes let out a cry and made the sign of the cross. Richard's gash was stitched at the hospital, where the doctors told the family that the boy would be alright.

This was his second serious head injury. Research by Ryan Darby, MD, assistant professor of Neurology at Vanderbilt University Medical Center (VUMC), shows brain lesions in a particular brain network may increase the risk of criminal behavior. This is referred to as acquired sociopathy.

This pattern of brain trauma is seen in other well-known murderers. Edmund Kemper, John Wayne Gacy, Jerry Brudos, Gary Heidnik, and Ed Gein are all serial killers who suffered from brain lesions, which is abnormal brain tissue resulting from trauma, brain tumor, or strokes. According to Darby, the morality, values, and reward and punishment decision-making networks are affected by brain lesions in criminals. A 2014 study published in the journal *Aggression and Violent Behavior* revealed that slightly over 20 percent of 239 serial and mass murderers examined had suffered head injuries in childhood. Richard was unlucky enough to have suffered two. Although, brain injury alone isn't enough to create a serial killer. Other influences are at play—influences Richard fell under as he matured.

It wasn't until fifth grade the extent of damage from Richard's head injuries was revealed. To the other students, no one saw anything unordinary in Richard. He was funny, and had the other students laughing all the time. Many of the girls considered him good-looking and nice. He would wait and walk with Patricia Kassfy to school and back. They had some rough neighborhoods to pass through, and Richard was sure to be there to watch out for his friend. "Richard was very sweet, quiet—in a way shy," Patricia recalled. "Because we lived on the same block, I saw him just about every day. He kind of watched over me. Made sure nobody bothered me. He was a good-looking boy. The girls liked him. He was nice."

And Patricia was there during the first seizure at school. She sat behind Richard, who was always turning around to crack jokes. But this day was different. He spun around in his seat, and the math teacher yelled at him. He slunk down in his chair, but that was normal behavior. Perhaps he was pouting for being caught or trying to escape the teacher's gaze. But Richard slid lower until he fell out of his seat and onto the floor. He cursed loudly as his body was overrun with convulsions. The teacher instructed the students to get up and look out the window. A frightened Patricia was sent to retrieve the school nurse. She'd never seen an epileptic seizure like that before.

Mercedes was phoned at work. She wasted not one second arriving at the school. There she found Richard in the nurse's office, lying down. He was visibly shaken and upset. He had no memory of the event and insisted that he was fine. He didn't want to lie down and sleep. It was a beautiful, sunny day, and Richard wanted to be out playing with his friends. He wanted to forget the whole episode at school.

The second epileptic seizure happened the very next day. He fell down in front of the lockers, cursing and beginning to shake violently. This time, he was taken straight to the hospital, where Mercedes was told her son was epileptic and suffered from grand mal seizures.

Grand mal seizures are caused by abnormal electrical activity in the brain. There was no serious cause for concern. Mercedes was informed that Richard would most likely grow out of this later in life. No medication was prescribed, nor a second appointment scheduled. Richard and his mother were sent on their way.

The days passed and Richard would be caught by his family, staring off for long periods of time. These smaller seizures pulled him into his mind, cutting him off from the room and the people around him. He would stare, transfixed on something like the wall or floor for ten or fifteen minutes. He would not speak nor move.

Thankfully, in his teens, the seizures lessened. Richard Ramirez would later be diagnosed with temporal lobe epilepsy. There are a certain amount of people who suffer from this type of epilepsy who go on to experience a change in sexuality, are overcome with an intense desire to write, become hyper-religious, or develop serious aggression.

Young Richard would look out a window and see monsters running about, horrifying visions that haunted him. This was what experts later believed was a potential side effect of petit mal seizures. Richard and his family didn't know that then. Instead, they wrote it off as nothing more than the boy's vivid imagination. He had a fondness for horror movies and TV shows. He was the first child in the morning to get up and hurry to the television, where he'd sit up close, digging into a bowl of sugar-filled cereal.

Aside from the epilepsy, Richard was an average, good kid. He was disciplined from time to time for joking too much, but otherwise, he was fairly normal. He had friends and was active. Until 1973, he did well in school. Then he reached the seventh grade. His grades took a serious hit. Richard's marks were barely passing. His parents feared he would follow the same course as his older brothers.

Robert and Ruben were both in the class at Bowie Junior High School for students with learning disabilities. Mr. Frank McMan was the instructor of the class. He had dark hair and a reddish tone to his complexion. To most, Frank came across as someone with a deep concern for his students and their learning. He worked with the struggling students and seemed to go out of his way to be helpful.

But the reality of their teacher was much more horrifying.

Frank McMan was a child molester who abused dozens of children he taught. None of his students spoke about their teacher's dark desires. They had to be frightened, afraid speaking up would result in getting in trouble. If an adult was telling them to do certain things, children were taught they should listen without question.

Frank went as far as to stop in at the Ramirez household for visits under the guise he was there to help with schoolwork. He developed a keen liking for both Ruben and Robert, and while Julian and Mercedes were at work, he would come over. There, he abused the boys.

Robert later described their relationship with the teacher. "He would come over to our house in the afternoon, do things, and take us back to his place. Like a couple of times a week, for a while. My mother and father knew [about the visits], but we told them we were doing work for him at his house and that he was helping us with schoolwork. But he was sucking our cocks and getting us off … He would even give us blow jobs in the bathroom at school. It felt good; what the fuck—so I never told anyone."

Richard spent time with McMan outside of school as well. Whether or not he was abused, he claimed to not remember. He would have been around seven years old at the time. What Richard did recall was a pedophile who lived near his home on Sapian Street. He professed to have witnessed this man rape a boy by inserting a candlestick into the boy's rectum. The man continued aggressively sodomizing him. Richard left unable to witness the horror anymore as the young boy screamed.

Ruben continued furthering his criminal career. He stole vehicles and broke into people's homes. Every arrest forced Julian to pay for more expensive lawyers. The costs quickly added up. Within three years, Julian had to sell all three properties he'd bought with the money from laying track to afford Ruben's legal fees. Julian blamed marijuana and pills as toxic influences over the boys in the neighborhood. He also blamed his nephew Miguel, called Mike by his friends and family. Mike was known as a wrecking ball around Ledo street. He was young and tough, beating anyone he fought into the ground no matter their size. Nothing could stop him. Julian instructed his sons to avoid their cousin, who also inherited the infamous Ramirez hot and wild temper. Julian's warnings did nothing. He was not home enough to enforce his rules. It took the Vietnam War draft to pull Mike away from his family and friends in 1965.

The three older boys moved out before finishing high school. Ruben dropped out in eleventh grade and Robert during tenth. They wanted nothing to do with their father's hard rule over their lives. For the older boys, living with Julian was unbearable. Ruben got an apartment with friends out in El Paso, and Robert and Joseph got their own place together. But when Joseph graduated from high school, he went on to move in with his high school sweetheart in Arizona.

At nine years old, Richard and Ruth were now the only two children at home. Richard played on his own often. He had no trouble amusing himself for hours at a time.

He was tall for his age, with thick dark hair and deep brown eyes. Richard was an excellent athlete as well. He was quick on his feet. At Lincoln School, Richard was the quarterback for the football team. Every Saturday game Julian could attend without missing work, he went. He would watch, sitting in the stands and cheering as his youngest son played.

Richard loved playing football, and he was good at it. It gave him confidence, but all that changed one Saturday when a grand mal seizure struck. Without any remorse, the coach pulled Richard off the field and then off the team. He wouldn't be held liable for anything happening to the boy. It wasn't his problem to deal with, and Richard was too much of a risk. Being kicked off the team gravely upset Richard. His epilepsy wasn't his fault. It wasn't fair. It was during this time that Ruth first noticed a shift in her brother's quiet but docile personality. Something darker loomed beneath the surface.

Cousin

Up until his cousin's return, Richard had been a rather normal child. He had the occasional outburst or upset, but this was normal and to be expected especially for the Ramirez family. He had developed into a bit of a loner, but was still considered a nice kid. Ray Garcia, a childhood friend, told investigators later that Richard hung around the arcades to play video games or went to the local 7-11 store to pass his time.

All of that changed when Mike came home.

After two tours, cousin Miguel returned from the Vietnam War a decorated soldier and war hero. The family, including Julian, was proud of this accomplishment. Miguel had served his country and done it well. While serving, he and another fellow soldier were the only two out of a platoon of twenty Green Berets to make it out alive. They had been surrounded by a group of Vietnamese. His arrival home came with four shining medals pinned to his chest. Miguel told Richard he had twenty-nine kills to his name. He'd thrived in guerilla-style warfare. Miguel had finally unleashed his rage and anger, and on the battlefield, he'd received copious amounts of praise for it.

When American soldiers learned the Vietnamese believed having a mutilated body part prevented them from entering heaven, the American soldiers went out of their way to maim them. Many Americans wore necklaces of human ears around their necks. Rape happened frequently. It was part of the war and Miguel had his fair share. Mike seized every opportunity to rape the women in the villages he toured through. One time, he took a series of photos showing a woman being forced to perform oral sex on him. He held the cold steel of a .45 against her head. The last picture was with Mike standing tall, a giant grin plastered across his face, and in his hand was the decapitated head of the woman.

To twelve-year-old Richard, his cousin was nothing short of a real-life superhero. He'd gone to war and returned stronger. He saw how everyone respected Mike now. But the fact was, Mike's experience in Vietnam had transformed an already loose cannon into a firing gun. For cousin Mike, violence was the key to becoming God-like. There was to be no mercy. Richard consumed this belief and everything Mike threw at him, absorbing it like a sponge. Richard later explained what his cousin told him about killing. "Having power over life and death was a high, an incredible rush. It was godlike. You controlled who'd live and who died—you were God." Mike had already been quite a bad influence on the older Ramirez boys. Now he'd captured another, but this time, he was far more dangerous.

Mike shared the disturbing photos he'd taken while in Vietnam with his impressionable young cousin. They were stored in his closet safely in a shoebox, the edges worn from the constant handling. He also kept a suitcase with shrunken heads under his bed. Miguel showed Richard these photos over and over. He believed they proved his power and god-like status. For Richard, the images imprinted a lasting stamp.

His innocent mind absorbed these gruesome pictures, for he viewed them while just beginning puberty. He didn't know why, but they excited and aroused him greatly. Even though he knew it was wrong, he masturbated thinking of them. Jesus and the Catholic God he grew up worshiping would frown upon such behavior, but the creeping idea Satan would accept him began to rise through Richard. Why should he stay with a religion that would despise his wants and desires?

Miguel never received proper help for transitioning back to normal life. His mental state remained locked in the gears for war. He married a strong Mexican-American woman, Jessie, with whom he had two sons.

Without Richard's two older brothers around, Mike took it upon himself to show his younger cousin the ways of the world. Richard was now completely under his cousin's wing. They spent a lot of their time driving around El Paso, smoking weed. Richard had started smoking when he was ten years old. His older brothers and sister all smoked marijuana. Frances Bustillos, who grew up in the same neighborhood as Richard, remembered his use of weed. "I don't think he knew what he was doing half the time. Whenever I saw him, he was really stoned."

Mike and Richard jammed to the radio as he filled Richard's head with dark stories about Vietnam and his sexually sadistic escapades. He taught Richard how to fight, how to kill stealthily and not leave a trace. Richard took in all the information eagerly. With a young, malleable mind, the youngest Ramirez was already angry at the world and his position within it. Mike gave him the gift of brutality and the notion to take what you want through savagery.

Julian gave up on keeping Richard away from his cousin. No punishment could stop him from spending all his time with Mike.

Richard was as stubborn as a dog with a bone. Anytime his father attempted to enforce a punishment, he ran quickly. Joseph described how the encounters went: "Fast like a rabbit before my father even moved in his direction."

To escape Julian's anger, Richard spent many nights in Cordova Cemetery. Sleeping bag tucked tightly under his arm, Richard hurried out of the house. He found peace and security in the cemetery where many kids found fear. Richard relished the quiet nights under the open sky and white stars, and in the morning, he could return home unscathed after his father left for work.

On May 4, 1973, Richard spent a typical day with his cousin at Miguel's home. In the late afternoon, they were hanging out, playing a game of miniature pool. Mike's wife, Jessie, was off grocery shopping that afternoon, so it was a day for the guys. Jessie was exhausted with her husband and his lifestyle. All he did now was lift weights, smoke pot, and reminisce about the war. She kept on him about getting a job and to stop hanging out with his kid cousin. They had two children of their own, and he was not pulling his weight. Mike couldn't care less about what his wife wanted.

In the middle of the game, Richard went to the fridge to grab himself a can of Coke. There on the top shelf was Mike's .38-caliber with a two-inch barrel sitting in the cold refrigerator air. Richard asked his cousin immediately about the pistol. "Hey! What's that doing in the refrigerator?"

Nonchalantly, Mike responded, "I may be using it, and I want it to be cool." The comment did little to explain the gun in the fridge to Richard, but he was about to find out.

Soon afterward, Jessie came home, groceries in hand, along with their two children. Immediately, she brought up issues of not having enough money and how Mike needed to get a job. Mike was quick to snap back. He planned to get a job, but not yet. He wasn't ready for one. He told his wife to shut up and stop the whiny bullshit. He was done with it all. But she didn't stop. She continued harping him.

That was it.

He got up from his seat calmly, went to the kitchen, and opened the refrigerator door. In his hand, he clutched the loaded pistol. Mike turned and pointed it directly at his wife. No ounce of fear was visible on her face. Instead, she wanted to know what the hell he planned to do with that gun. He said he was going to shoot her if she didn't stop her nagging. Jessie squared her feet and stuck her chin out. She dared her husband to shoot her.

Mike lifted the gun and fired. He shot his wife point-blank in the face.

The bullet cleared, hitting right above her lip and exiting the back of her head. *Smack*. Richard watched in utter shock as his cousin's wife slammed lifeless onto the floor of her home. Deep red blood pooled from her shaking body as the last seconds of her life ended. Richard's ear rang from the close impact. The smell of fresh death and smoke filled the little apartment. The cries of Mike's two scared children poured out. He turned to face the dumbstruck Richard. "You don't *ever* say you saw this!" he snapped quickly. "You understand?"

In a daze, completely stunned, Richard walked home to Ledo street under the afternoon sun. He didn't know how to process witnessing the cold-blooded murder. He later claimed to not have been traumatized by the incident, only shocked. He was greatly upset, yet he followed Mike's instruction. Perhaps out of fear or sheer respect, he would tell no one of what he saw that day. Not even his sister, Ruth.

Julian arrived home from work in the evening, and right before supper that night, the phone rang. Julian answered. It was Mike's mother, Victoria, calling. She told him about the shooting and asked for his help down at the police station. Mike's father had passed away several years ago, and as his uncle, Julian had to take on the role of father. Even with his negative attitude toward Mike, Julian had a duty to the family and agreed to come.

Richard remained silent as his father hung up the phone and told the family the news. They assumed he was upset over his cousin's arrest and charge for murder. Little did they know what Richard had seen that day.

Several days after the murder, Julian received a call from his nephew in prison. Mike needed a favor from the family. He had been thriving in prison. It was a do-or-die lifestyle, and he fit in perfectly. He called his uncle to ask for someone to swing by his apartment and pick up several pieces of jewelry.

Richard went with his parents that hot, late afternoon to Mike's apartment. Julian opened the door to find the pool of Jessie's

43

blood. He stared at the bloodstain, then quickly told his wife to stay in the car. But Richard was instructed to come help search for the jewelry. They walked inside the apartment. It was quiet and stale. Richard described the scene: "The stillness of the room, the eeriness, you know. We had to open the windows to ventilate the room and it was something. It was … [long pause] … it was death! I had known the woman. I had known her very well."

Julian bent down and scooped up the slug that had killed Jessie. It had hit the wall and fallen to the floor after blasting through her. He and Richard both marveled at the power of the bullet and the damage it had inflicted.

Richard and his father began to rummage through the belongings, looking for the jewelry. He rifled through her purse looking at her ID cards and personal things. It was then that a flip switched in Richard's mind. Being in the house and going through Jessie's things after she'd just been violently murdered was like no other feeling he'd known. It gave him a bolt of power. Julian and Richard grabbed the jewelry and returned to the waiting Mercedes.

Richard never told his parents that he'd witnessed the shooting. But he later described revisiting the apartment with his dad and the lasting effect it had on the twelve-year-old's young, impressionable mind. "That day I went back to that apartment, it was like some kind of mystical experience. It was all quiet and still and hot in there. You could smell the dried blood. Particles of dust just seemed to hover in the air. I looked at the place where Jessie had fallen and died, and I got this kind of tingly feeling. It was the strangest thing. Then my father told me to look in her pocketbook for this jewelry my cousin wanted, and I dumped Jessie's pocketbook on the bed and looked through her things. It gave me the weirdest feeling— I mean, I knew her, and these were her things, and she was dead. Murdered. Gone. And I was touching her things. It made me feel … in contact with her."

That was the first real close encounter with death Richard experienced. He claimed, "Ever since, I was intrigued."

The City of Sex and Sin

"Just stay here at the house. You don't have to do anything. Just let me go to work in peace, with a clear mind that you are here and not in any kind of trouble. Please," Julian pleaded with Richard. No matter how much he fought his son, Richard would not listen. Not after Jessie's death. Something had clicked in the boy. He withdrew more and more from the family, losing all interest in school. Without Mike, he lost direction and purpose. He smoked more weed and began to steal, breaking into homes. His black, curly hair was grown out along the sharp lines of his cheekbones. All his time was spent smoking dope, every day and into the night with Ruth.

He left El Paso for the first time to spend the summer of 1972 with Ruben, who'd moved out to L.A. At twenty years old, Ruben's heroin abuse drove him out to the city of Angels with his wife, Suzanna. Ruben made his way by stealing and intertwining himself with the other criminals who hung around the bus terminal. Drugs and sex ran rampant. He associated himself with a group of Mexican-Americans who survived by breaking and entering into the expensive homes around L.A. to buy their next high.

When Richard made his way out there, Ruben had already fathered a baby boy. He hardly used heroin anymore, but he continued smoking weed and stealing.

Almost thirteen years old and standing five-foot-nine, Richard climbed onto the bus headed north. His father worried that without any real adult supervision, his youngest was under the complete care of Ruben. Since Richard had grown extremely reserved and withdrawn from the family after Mike's arrest, he and Mercedes thought a summer out of El Paso would be good for him. Mercedes made Ruben swear on the Sacred Heart of Jesus he would watch over his little brother. Her oldest made the promise over the phone. They wouldn't get in any trouble.

It was a lie.

Richard settled down on one of the stiff cushions. The bus ride was long and the seat uncomfortable, but he was far too excited to sleep through it. Ideas of wealth and vanity filled his head. He couldn't even begin to imagine what waited for him in Los Angeles.

Richard had developed a serious knack for stealing. Mike had taught him what he needed to know, and he'd broken into several homes on his own. The thrill of breaking in excited him. Richard

47

quickly harbored a love for walking around in a stranger's home in the late hours of the night. The intimacy of stepping through the hallways, going through the belongings, and taking their security felt powerful. Sexual fantasies of bondage danced in his young mind. Plus, there was easy money to be made. He'd seen his brothers and cousin do it enough, and now, he was desensitized to the stigma that breaking and entering was morally wrong. He didn't care if it went against the church and the Ten Commandments. Everyone around him did it. Plus, Richard was good at stealing, and he enjoyed it. Maybe too much.

Ruben waited at the terminal. They greeted one another fondly. Richard was happy to be away from his parents and out of the house. Together they lit up a joint to smoke while driving around the downtown area. Richard got the full tour. The tall buildings of the city were impressive, looming over Main. For the boy, it was all brand new and exciting. He'd never seen anything so impressive, and marveled at it all with wide eyes. But Ruben was sure to point out that the money was really found out in Beverly Hills, Malibu, and Bel Air. Those were the real scores.

For the first time, Richard visited the ocean. The sparkling blue water was stunning. He decided he'd never seen anything so beautiful in his life. But it was all the women walking past him in nothing more than skimpy bikinis that really drew Richard in. He watched them move around the beach, boldly showing skin. He couldn't believe the women out in L.A.

He quickly learned that summer what this city was really about—sin and sex, and a lot of it.

Even the prostitutes were bolder here. Not like the ones in Mexico, who were fairly reserved. Oh no. Here the women were half-dressed, moving their bodies, shaking their hips, bending forward for revealing glimpses of cleavage. They'd call out to their potential customers with bright red painted lips. With his height, Richard easily passed in and out of sex stores without raising a brow. It gave him access to the hardcore content he craved. He was excited by it all. All those bondage fantasies were finally considered normal in this setting. They were advertised openly. At twelve years old, Richard knew he had found his ideal place. He couldn't be judged here.

Ruben brought him along to burglarize homes several times during that summer trip. He taught Richard to perfect his art, picking locks, inspecting homes for alarms or other threats. Mike had laid a foundation and now Ruben gave Richard the last important details of break-ins.

That summer solidified it for Richard. He came home to El Paso with little regard for school. He made up his mind. Education was useless. Stealing provided far more value. The principal at Jefferson High remembered Richard during this time of transition. "He was not a bad boy, though he fell in with bad company. He played a lot of hooky. His grades were all failing. It was a shame because he was a smart young man. He just didn't seem to care; wouldn't apply himself. Richard seemed troubled."

Julian secretly prayed his son would succeed in school and excel in life. Richard was his last hope, but it was quickly fading. His youngest had no interest, even though he was noted as a smart student. The only subject Richard received high marks in was physical conditioning.

Outside of the classroom, Richard developed a love for hunting. Julian had taken him out, taught him to shoot. He went with the .22 rifle Julian gave him and stalked different prey in El Paso's vast desert. Richard was skilled at stalking the animals. He'd take them by surprise and savored digging his blade into their warm bodies to gut them. After the hunt, he came home, giving the entrails to the family dog, Indio, whom he loved dearly.

On Saturdays, Richard went to the cinema and watched all the horror movies playing. There he'd watch the triple feature. He mainly enjoyed the dark horror, never feeling afraid like the other moviegoers, who'd scream or turn away. When walking home, Richard would imagine he was the horrible monster from the movies inflicting fear. He took karate and then quit after learning the basics. On his own, he practiced punching and kicking for hours. Though Richard never sought out fights, he made sure he'd win them if the time ever came. He was thin but strong, and very fast, with a tall, lean structure of sinewy muscle. He even had the Ramirezes' strong, large hands to strike powerful blows with.

Julian continued struggling with keeping his youngest son disciplined. The two butted heads constantly. Eventually, Richard decided he could take no more from his strict father's rule, and at thirteen years old, he decided to temporarily move in with his sister Ruth and her new husband Roberto Avala, whom Julian did not approve of.

51

Roberto Avala was a handsome, strong, Mexican-American man. For Ruth, marriage provided her with the opportunity to escape her father's household in a more amicable manner than her brothers. She wasn't simply leaving; she was a wife now and was starting her own family. But problems quickly rose in the marriage. Roberto had an extremely high libido and was a habitual pervert. He demanded sex from his wife constantly. After they would have sex, he often slinked off into the night to find windows to peer through, hoping to find a naked woman or other people engaged in sex. Sometimes, he would even tell Ruth what he saw. She'd laughed it off in the beginning, but soon enough, his obsession with voyeurism got out of hand. Roberto would rather watch young women through their windows, than have sex with his wife. The fights between the two of them began, and the household was in a constant state of turmoil.

Roberto decided to share his nightly sneaking habits with Richard during the summer of '73. He showed what houses to visit and at what times. He had the whole neighborhood layout mapped out. Richard took to it immediately. Sneaking around was sexually exciting and thrilling. He learned the best peeping spots and how to avoid being caught. It was only a matter of time until Ruth uncovered what her husband and little brother were up to in the late hours of the night. She threatened to divorce Roberto unless serious changes were made.

Roberto didn't stop, and after two years of marriage, Ruth left her husband.

Richard and Ruth continued to live together. Even with Roberto gone, the younger boy never stopped sneaking out on late adventures. He continued to watch people, and several times went as far as to sneak into their homes in the dead of night while the occupants unknowingly slept, just to know he could do it.

During this time, Richard dove deeper into using drugs. He experimented with hallucinogens, tripping on acid. He used magic mushrooms and peyote, common drugs found around El Paso. Richard was restless, the type to never sleep. He enjoyed the night and its darkness. This was the time he found he came alive, like a vampire. And under the influence of drugs, he'd stay out in the desert, hunting by the white moonlight. Richard believed Satan would come to him then and they would communicate. Satan had become a prominent figure in Richard's life, one he conjured in his head. Satan didn't judge Richard for his dark desires. This gave Richard a means to justify his nightmarish acts. What he did, he did for Satan. He withdrew more from his friends, who noticed a visible change in Richard; later, one good friend would admit he believed Richard took a sharp turn when he began messing with harder drugs. The boy continued to stay close with Ruth and Joseph.

During this period, he developed his intense love for heavy metal. He listened incessantly to AC/DC, Judas Priest, Billy Idol, and any other band that was considered wild for the time. He believed they promoted evil with their music and Satan. For Richard, it was another justification for choosing to become a monster. He used their music as inspiration.

Satan's Disciple

Richard took his first job when he was fifteen years old, at a Holiday Inn. It was easy, light maintenance work. He carried luggage and helped clean. But to Richard, the best part of work was the myriad attractive women who came and went. He'd fantasize about them, masturbating to the ideas of tying them up. First, he made a pass at one, letting her know he thought she was attractive. She immediately told her parents about the young worker who had gotten friendly, and Richard was reprimanded promptly. He promised not to hit on any more of the guests. He would be fired if a similar incident were to ever happen again. The manager had Richard apologize to the parents, and it was forgotten.

Three months passed without another mishap. But in the meantime, Richard had obtained a master key from a recently fired. Unbeknownst to management or the customers, Richard peered through the windows to catch glimpses of the guests. The curtains, when drawn, left just enough of a narrow gap for Richard to spy through. But now he had the key. He entered their rooms with ease, where he'd find the valuables lying about, ripe for the taking or he'd slip into the closet to hide, watching women undress.

He would wait, listening through the window to ensure the guests were fast asleep. When the coast was clear, he slipped into their rooms with the master key and dropped to the floor, waiting to see if the guests were disturbed by the intrusion—just as his cousin Mike had taught him. When he was in the clear, he stayed low, moving among the room to sift through wallets and collect anything of value.

Richard went for months between his breaking and entering. He was quiet and discreet and went completely unnoticed. No one ever suspected him, leaving the police and the staff baffled about the random occurrences of theft.

He continued his prowling around the hotel, but his sexual desires grew. He wanted to do more than watch the women from their windows or closets. He wanted to fulfill his fantasies. One night, he took the plunge. He picked out his first victim: a twenty-year-old woman with dark hair and a curvy figure. Twisted ideas began to evolve in his mind. He had plans to blindfold, bind, and have his way with her.

One a.m. rolled around. Richard peeked in the window of his chosen victim. He saw her all alone in her room in nothing more than an unbuttoned nightshirt, her bra, and underwear. Perfect. She slipped into the bathroom, and Richard used the master key to enter her room. Like a cat, quick and silent, he slinked in and hid within her closet. The element of surprise was a necessary part of his plan. He waited for her to walk in front of the closet. He'd strike from behind.

Then his moment came. When her back was turned, he leaped from the closet, tackling her. His hand grasped tightly over her mouth. He brought her to the floor, gagging her with her underwear. He told her not to scream, nor to turn and look at him.

Richard moved to tie her up. He was moments away from his dark desires finally coming true. He began to attempt to have sex with her. But the hotel door flew open.

The woman's husband entered, immediately enraged by the sight. He had merely stepped out of the room to grab a bite to eat. He was a big man, especially compared to the young Richard who was 120 pounds at the time. The husband did nothing to hold back. Like a massive wall, he rammed into Richard, knocking him to the floor. He used his thick fists to beat Richard until he was bloodied and unconscious. The man then untied his wife and called the front desk. They wasted no time contacting the police.

Richard was so badly beaten the police brought him to the hospital. Both of his eyes were black, and his face swollen and bruised. He received treatment for a concussion and a few stitches. He was lying on the gurney in handcuffs when his sister and mother arrived to find him. He was hardly recognizable, he'd been beaten so brutally. They couldn't fathom their sweet Richard would ever commit such a horrid act.

The boy made sure to spin his story. He told his mother the woman had come onto him and then her husband, in a jealous fit, beat him. He had been nothing more than an innocent victim to it all.

His mother and sister believed him without question. They were deeply in denial. The Richard they knew was far too sweet and kind to attempt to rape a young woman.

He was fifteen, and the judge treated him as such. He was released to his mother that night. The man and woman were from out of state and only wanted to forget the horrible event. They would never return to El Paso. The whole night was to be forgotten.

At the time, Ruben was out in Los Angeles. Robert had gotten into a fight over a traffic incident and was spending time in an Arizona prison. Joseph had two children and had gotten his left leg amputated at the knee. Richard's three older brothers were out of his life, and his relationship with his own father was absent.

After four-and-a-half years, Mike was released from Texas State Mental Hospital in late 1977. He had been assessed with suffering from posttraumatic stress disorder, and the doctors believed he deserved a second chance. The war was what drove him to kill his wife. He didn't have proper rehabilitation back into the world, but now, he was ready. He and Richard immediately began spending more time together like they had when Richard was twelve. Without his older brothers around, Mike was Richard's role model and continued to fill the role of mentor. They spent their time driving around, getting high. They never spoke about Jessie's death. Aside from his older cousin, Richard rarely saw or spent time with other people.

The sixteen-year-old earned himself the nickname of "Dedos" or "Fingers." He'd become quite the adept thief, waiting in the dark hours of the morning to slip into homes around El Paso dressed in all black. He took as much as he could possibly carry. "He had this disease," Ray Garcia said to investigators. "Things would stick to his fingers. We used to call him Ricky the Klepto." Without his father knowing, Richard sold almost everything he stole.

Teachers took note of Richard's long absences and his frequent cutting class. He slept through most of the lessons and constantly looked exhausted. There was no effort to participate, simply to get through the school day.

But all these nightly runs were nothing more to Richard than practice for the day he would return to Los Angeles. He knew that there was where the real prizes awaited him. If he wasn't burglarizing homes, then he continued to stalk the wildlife in the desert, taking hallucinogens during his outings. He saw horrifying monsters while high who did what they wanted and took from people, terrorizing them.

Richard continued to keep the dark side of him hidden from others.

With curly blonde hair and a sweet smile, fifteen-year-old Nancy Avila had never stopped thinking about Richard Ramirez. The first time she'd seen him she was only twelve, but she never got him out of her head. He was, after all, quite handsome. She lived across the street a few houses down from the Ramirezess and would catch glimpses of Richard every once in a while when he came to visit his mother at Ledo Street. Finally, she approached him one day after mustering the courage to cross the street. They chatted casually for a bit. That one conversation was all it took. Nancy was hooked.

After that day, she couldn't get Richard out of her mind. She was completely infatuated. She called him and the two began to talk on the phone regularly. They finally met one night to sneak off to the cemetery that Richard used as an escape from his father. He had a blanket laid out beneath a tree, and the two would make love. Nancy heard rumors about Richard being a thief, but she brushed it off as nothing more than jealous lies. Later, Nancy told a reporter when asked if Richard forced anything on her, "Oh, no, never anything like that! I was willing and we just did it. I felt guilty sometimes, but I still did it. I was young and I really loved him and I thought he loved me. There was something very different about Richard; he had an aura about him that just drew me in. He was generous and he was fun."

Their relationship ended in the new year. Nancy wanted to spend more time with Richard, but she was young and a good girl. She couldn't give Richard what he really wanted.

Richard had outgrown El Paso. It was time for him to finally answer his true calling. Mike had remarried and developed an addiction to heroin.

Richard dropped out of high school at seventeen. FBI records show he was arrested three times after dropping out. The first two charges were for marijuana possession. The final was for reckless driving. That time, Richard was driving around in a friend's car when he was stopped. On the passenger seat sat a toy cap gun, a ski mask, and a green wallet. The wallet was stolen, plucked right out of a woman's handbag, but she was unable to identify the theft. The reckless driving charge was dropped. But the two accounts of marijuana possession gave Richard three years of probation.

He had no plans of sticking around afterward.

In February of 1978, Richard climbed onto the Greyhound bus headed for Los Angeles.

All of his belongings were contained in a black knapsack. He had a plan to sell weed purchased for dirt cheap in El Paso for a lot more out in L.A. He hadn't told anyone about his move. He was eighteen now and an adult.

On the bus he slipped his headphones on, listening to his favorite heavy metal songs. Richard had now fully renounced the Catholic church and accepted Satan. Satan didn't judge like Jesus Christ. Richard believed the devil would protect him while he robbed the wealthy. It would only be a matter of time until Richard Ramirez would live in a mansion with a horde of women who were his slaves, serving his every whim. These were the images he fantasized about. This was what Richard believed L.A. would give him.

Richard hopped off the rusty, old Greyhound and walked to the main street. He passed by half-dressed hookers with missing teeth and coke addicts strung out in the shadows of the sidewalk. L.A. was what Richard considered Satan's city. The first day, he headed straight to an adult bookstore and bought the dirtiest magazine on bondage he could find. He settled in for the night in one of the hotels in Skid Row. He was home now. He spent his time in dirty, seedy bars filled with smoke and slept in hotels, selling his weed for extra money. For Richard, this was where he belonged. Where no one judged him or told him what to do. He could live the life he pleased.

At times, he would often visit Ruben and Suzanna, but the visits ended after a brutal fight between the two brothers. Ruben accused him of coming onto his wife. Whether or not Ruben was right in his accusations, Richard stopped visiting.

His first year in L.A., Richard spent a lot of his time gambling. He was never seen dating women or even really around them. Most of his money went to shooting craps. His interests were elsewhere. But the gambling stopped when Richard became extremely addicted to cocaine. It was the eighties, and the drug was extremely popular. Unlike with other people, for Richard, it was more than just getting high. Cocaine made him feel powerful, opened up the dark recess of his mind, and brought him closer to Satan. He injected it, giving him a more intense and direct high. Mainlining cocaine creates a quick and powerful high, lasting merely five to ten minutes, making it very habit-forming. Under its influence, Richard was supercharged with an incredible boost to focus, and his confidence skyrocketed. But the high can be accompanied by agitation, aggression, and induced psychosis.

Highly addicted, Richard committed a score of burglaries every week to scrape together around $1,500 to provide for his cocaine habit. His regular fences near the terminal eagerly purchased what he'd bring them. Richard would in turn take the money to get his needed high. His time was spent breaking and entering, injecting cocaine, and developing a stronger relationship with Satan. He believed cocaine brought him closer to the devil, intensifying his violent, twisted desires even more. He'd lost all want for a normal sexual relationship, and his need turned solely toward violent rape fantasies. Sadism became more a part of Richard's sexuality. Access to dark bondage porn only increased Richard's desire.

Fifteen months after the day Richard moved to L.A., he was living in stolen cars. He would hotwire a vehicle or slip in while the owner paid for gas. Each stolen car gave Richard a home for several days. Then he'd dump it somewhere only to scoop up another ride. For hours, Richard would drive along the roads. He scoured the area, memorizing the maps and routes. Ideas of what grand homes he'd rob next laid out in his mind during these trips. He scouted and planned, sleeping in the car with the seat fully reclined.

The local merchants around where Richard hung out took note of him. He came across as nervous and on edge. His clothing was always dark in color, with sunglasses over his eyes and an AC/DC baseball cap pulled down to shade his face. He spoke constantly about his affinity for heavy metal and particular bands he listened to. He ate a lot at a restaurant called the Fat Brat for breakfast, a fast-food joint. The owner noticed how Richard was never afraid to spend a lot of cash.

Stealing was his way of taking what he believed he was entitled to. To Richard, America's system was skewed. His family worked and slaved away to have so little when these people had so much. In his mind, everything he stole was justified. He was balancing the system and taking what he deserved all along.

Soon, it was a hot summer night in 1978. Richard had started using PCP, a powerful narcotic known to induce serious bouts of psychosis and anger.

With the use of angel dust came Richard's second act of violence.

He was hanging around Spring Street when a pretty brunette approached him. She was looking for some angel dust. Richard agreed to cop her some, and together they made their way back to her apartment. They smoked the drug, letting the high take over. For most individuals, the high of PCP feels as though there is a loss of control in their mind. Often this results in violent and impulsive behaviors. As if primary urges take over, reactions are inevitable.

Richard came onto the woman. She immediately turned him down, letting him know she was a lesbian and he shouldn't even waste his time making a move. Anger surged through Richard. He was not about to be rejected like that. He would have her one way or another. Three a.m. came. The drugs ran out. She told Ramirez it was time to go. He exited the apartment into the stairwell, and instead of leaving, he made his way to the roof of the building. Underneath the dark night sky, he waited patiently. The apartment light went out, and Richard carefully descended the fire escape to the woman's window, which he had unlocked earlier. It was time for him to act.

Surprise and fear took over the woman. Richard covered her eyes immediately, gagging her. She did everything she could to try and fight him, but it was no use. Richard tied her up. His blood boiled with desire. Several times he raped her. He left when the sun broke the horizon. He'd successfully acted out one of his fantasies. It was thrilling and the enjoyment was addictive. Vile ecstasy filled him.

Several days passed after the assault and Richard came across Anton LaVey's *The Satanic Bible*. LaVey's teachings filled Richard's mind with grand ideas. He took in every word with serious conviction. Finally, he'd found someone who shared the same feelings toward Satan. Richard was understood. In a stolen car, he made the trip to San Francisco to be among other Satan worshippers. He wanted to meet LaVey and attend one of the Church of Satan's services opened to the public.

Richard watched as a ceremony was done over the body of a naked woman. It was then he felt a hand, cold as ice, grip his shoulder. He felt the presence of the devil. Richard called his mother after returning to L.A., asking her to pray for him. "I was touched by Satan tonight, Mama. He came to me."

Richard continued consuming more of LaVey's work. He agreed with it all and from then proclaimed himself to be a true and devoted Satanist. He described his acceptance later on in an interview. "It was about 1980, and I was hustling on the streets. I landed in jail for a month or two for petty theft. I met up with this guy who was a Satan worshiper. For those two months, I was with him, then I get out of jail, but my mind didn't. I remembered everything he said, which basically was, 'Why worship the good guy when the things you do aren't so good?' Somehow it just made sense to me, to worship something that would protect you in what you were doing."

Fully committed to his chosen path, Richard forwent personal hygiene altogether, never brushing his teeth and solely eating food from convenience stores. Acquaintance Mike Little remembered Richard at the time. "I could not take his lifestyle. First thing in the morning, he would roll a joint. He smoked lots of pot … He would buy those big Hershey bars and eat one after another," Little recalled. "He ate a lot of candy and potato chips and drank a lot of Cokes. I would take him to a restaurant so he could eat, but he wouldn't touch his food." The smell of wet weather began to follow Richard wherever he went like a hazy fog surrounding him. Mike Little noticed as well. "He was a pig … He never combed his hair or took a bath. And I never saw him brush his teeth."

To his family, it was clear Richard was heading down a treacherous path. Ruth made the journey out to L.A. in a bid to plead with her younger brother. She'd always had a soft spot for him. She took a bus from Texas up to L.A. for a visit. She had the goal to bring him back to Texas. But it was a hopeless attempt. Ruth arrived to find her brother. She pleaded with him, begging for his return. With cold evil lurking in his eyes, he responded to Ruth by blasting AC/DC's *Highway to Hell.* His voice rang out as he proclaimed his devotion to Satan, then injected himself with cocaine. He had what he needed, and it was not his family.

The perfect storm had brewed for a murderer. The Richard Ruth had known and loved was far gone. The time spent with his cousin and brothers, mixed with drug use and several brain traumas, had done its damage. Richard was ripe with the ingredients to commit murder.

It was only a matter of time.

Richard was never one to stay put for very long. He was a drifter at heart, always on the move. The San Francisco visit was a pleasant one for Richard. He liked the city and through the early eighties would often find his way back for periods of time. He moved back and forth between the cities. In San Francisco, he spent his time around the Tenderloin District. There he made friends among the shady characters that thrived in the high-crime-rate neighborhood.

Though Richard Ramirez's first charged crime happened in the summer of 1984, in 2009, cold case detective Holly Pera linked his DNA to the murder of nine-year-old Mei Leung. Holly Pera had been a young officer at the time, and she never forgot the horrific murder. It was one of the first cold cases she pulled. "I pulled the Mei Leung case because I remembered it from my days as a patrol officer when I was at Northern Station."

The night of April 10, 1984, Richard Ramirez left his spot dressed in all black. He usually stayed at 373 Ellis St. and 56 Mason St. during his visits to San Francisco, both of which were in the Tenderloin, six blocks away. He made his way out under the night sky and headed to the five-story apartment building at 765 O'Farrell. Cloaked in the thick of night, he loomed around, watching. He'd broken into many buildings like this. Close to home, he'd been able to keep an eye out. Perhaps he planned to spend the night burglarizing, or maybe the idea of murder spun through his mind early on.

At the same exact time, nine-year-old Mei Leung was returning home from a nearby friend's home with her eight-year-old brother, Mike. Mei was a sweet young girl with bright eyes and a charming smile. She had come with her mother, a restaurant worker, from Hong Kong along with her two sisters and brother in 1980. Together they approached the building steps when a dollar bill fell from Mei's pocket onto the ground. She realized she'd lost the dollar

71

and told her brother to head upstairs to their home. She wanted to stay and look for her dollar near the elevator. The bill might have blown under the basement door. Mike thought little of it and took the elevator up to their apartment without telling anyone what Mei was doing.

Not much is known about what exactly happened in the brief moments Mei searched for the dollar. Only fifteen to thirty minutes passed, but in that time, Richard Ramirez got his hands around Mei. Down in the basement, he brutally attacked her. He stabbed and raped her, finishing by strangulation.

Upstairs, Mei's mother noticed her daughter wasn't home yet. Mike went down to the basement to look for her. He found a terrible sight. His sister was half-naked, hanging from a drainpipe by her blouse. Blood dripped down onto the floor in a puddle. Inspector Ronald Schneider recalled the positioning of her body: "If you can picture Christ on the cross, that's the way she looked. Her head was dropped and her chin down." To many, it was believed this crime was an act of a satanic ritual.

Shortly after, a mother and her young son headed down to the basement. Perhaps they planned to switch over their laundry, but her son spotted the red blood left on the floor. She immediately hurried up the stairs to call the police and report it. With her son, they got on the elevator, where a young man stood. She took note of him as he fiddled with the controls as though he had no idea what he was doing.

In 2009, the police would later uncover not only Ramirez's DNA, but what they believed was a second suspect involved with the case.

Mei Leung is now known to be Richard's first murder and the catalyst for a crime spree so horrible, it would change the course of California.

The Hunters and Their Prey

Two grams. That was all it took for Robert to know exactly what his younger brother wanted. And Robert had clean, pure rock. He operated in the park right in front of the L.A. bus terminal.

On June 27, 1984, at 8:30 p.m., dressed in all black from head to toe including his socks, Richard hopped into the stolen dark-blue Toyota. He drove along the dirty roads he knew so well to an abandoned building off Pico Street. He wouldn't be bothered here. Richard knew all the spots. He would have preferred getting his high in one of the hotels for transients, where they didn't ask questions. But all the extra cash was spent on the next cocaine-driven high.

Under the summer night sky, Richard quickly pulled out two of the four little rocks from their makeshift aluminum foil wrapping. He was anxious. He placed the drugs in a half-cut Pepsi can, adding a little water, and waited as the cocaine quickly melted. He'd done this hundreds of times. Snatching the syringe, he kept it near so he could draw in the now-liquified cocaine. Richard tied his left arm tight with a cord right above the bicep. His veins raised and bulged. The

74

syringe pierced the swollen, thick vein after he removed the cord, and Richard injected himself with the drug.

The cocaine entered his system, pulsing with an electric wave. His senses were suddenly alert and the black pupils of his hollow eyes dilated. This was when Richard felt unstoppable.

He climbed back into the car, blasting heavy metal. The loud beats of the music stimulated him, empowered him as they carried dark messages of hell, hidden messages he understood were for him.

Over the course of that particular night, he returned to the same alley spot three times to inject himself with cocaine. He resumed driving around restlessly, his eyes scanning the streets. He thought about sex. Violent sex with hookers, but that took money. He would need more money if he wanted to get more cocaine. For Richard there was only one route—stealing.

The last of his high faded away, and as Richard came down, he was inflicted with agitated, jittery nerves. He turned onto the 10 Freeway, driving to the low-income community of Glassell Park. It was the perfect place for Richard to strike that night. He pulled his car over next to a cemetery and took a few moments to collect himself in the dim light. Then the dark gardening gloves slid over his hands. His eyes flickered around, ensuring no one was around to catch a glimpse of the shadow now hunting. Richard crept, avoiding the line of street lamps.

A two-story pink apartment building caught his eye. He took it in and walked around the building, studying the doors and windows. It wasn't well maintained, with five apartments on the second story and five on the ground floor. His eyes claimed apartment 2. It had a good escape route, and the window was open. Inside, seventy-nine-year-old Jennie Vincow slept.

Jennie had thinning, white hair, and stood at five-foot-nine. She'd moved out to warm California to be closer to her son, Jack, who lived in the apartment above hers in the same building. He wanted to be close to his elderly mother to check in on her often.

Richard approached the window. A tall, full tree covered the glass in shadow, blocking out the streetlight. For Richard, it didn't matter who resided in these walls. Satan was beside him, watching over him, ensuring that whatever dark acts needed to be done would be accomplished.

He removed a glove to better twist the screw of the window screen, then pulled it off, placing it down into the apartment. Ever so gently, he pushed the window open; then, in one swift motion, he hoisted himself up and in, landing silently. Richard waited for anyone to stir in the room, low to the ground. He blinked, letting his pupils dilate and adjust to the dark.

Immediately, anger twisted through Richard upon seeing how poor Jennie Vincow was. He'd picked the wrong apartment, and he was running out of time to score money for his next high. Rage continued to build inside of Richard. He turned on his pen light and began to search through Jennie's things. A suitcase at the end of the bed was empty of any valuables. He tried the dresser. She had no money, no jewelry, nothing of any worth to sell for drugs or sex.

His eyes snapped to the sleeping form of Jennie. Her chest rose and fell with each breath as she slept. The sight of her only made Richard's anger grow. He shook with venomous hate for her. His blood boiled hot, and his heart thudded deeply in his chest. A nasty snarl curled across Richard's lips.

Jennie Vincow was jolted awake by a six-inch hunting knife plunging into her chest. A guttural scream erupted from her. She tried to fight back, survival instincts taking over, but it was no use. Richard's massive hand clamped down like a lock over her mouth.

Arousal began to burn in Richard as he slid his blade across her neck, slicing ear to ear. The cut ran so deeply, he nearly decapitated Jennie. Her body convulsed as she choked, gagging on her own blood.

He didn't stop then, ripping back the blanket and thrusting the blade through her chest three more times. The motion sexually excited Richard even more. The act of it all, the red spilling blood that pooled into the bed sheets, leaving its permanent stain. The smell. Richard knew these brought him closer to Satan then. They were one, unified in the treacherous act.

Drugs had never made him feel like this. Richard stepped back, admiring his work. The thrill thrived under his skin. For one hour he stayed, consuming glass after glass of water. The air around him swirled with the scent of death and blood. He snatched a portable radio and stepped outside. The golden sun stretched its fingers along the horizon line, creeping up.

Around 5 a.m., he returned to the stolen car, his clothes still covered in Jennie's blood. He drove away, and at the corner of Weldon Avenue, he paused at a stop sign. His first reaction was to blow through it, but something told him not to, some instinct. Pulling away from the intersection, he saw it. The black and white paint of

LAPD cruiser, directly to his right. The cop watched Richard drive away in the stolen car, murder fresh on his hands.

Jack arrived at his mother's apartment around 1:20 p.m, ten hours after the brutal slaughter. He brought with him chicken nuggets from McDonald's. Jennie loved them, and he wanted to surprise her with lunch. He'd just finished fixing up the air conditioner in his car and thought they could go for a ride like Jennie enjoyed.

Upon arriving, the first thing Jack noticed was the missing screen on his mother's window. Odd. He took out his key only to find that the front door to her apartment was also unlocked. He opened the door. Blood was smeared along the walls and floor, and the screen of the window sat in the center of the living room floor.

A feeling of dread began to build in Jack. The apartment was still silent. The light in the bedroom was dark. He saw the form of his mother still in bed and slowly pulled back the blanket covering her. He saw the wounds, how her head was barely attached. He screamed out in horror, calling for help. He raced to the building's managers. "My mother's been murdered. Oh, God, please call the police!"

At 1:40 p.m., the police arrived. Jack waited under the hot sun in the front of the building. It was 96 degrees and sweltering. Tears streamed down his face as he paced in a frantic state of shock. Onlookers gathered around. Word of the murder had spread.

Lt. Buster Altizer was the first on the scene. He followed Jack into his mother's silent apartment. The smell of human death was pungent. Lt. Buster Altizer didn't need to examine much to know this was a murder, and a brutal, sadistic one at that. Yellow tape was strung up, and backup was called.

Homicide detective Jesse Castillo and his partner, Mike Wynn, showed up shortly after receiving the call. Even for seasoned detectives like Castillo, the site of murder was gruesome. They called in the team and began to investigate the crime. Upon pulling back the blanket covering Jennie, they immediately took in the gravity of the vile act. Wounds on her hands showed how she'd made the attempt to fight back against her attacker. Her blue nightgown, now saturated red with blood, had been shoved over up to her waist, and the crotch of her girdle cut out. She was taken away in a black body bag to the county morgue for an autopsy.

The LAPD fingerprint expert arrived on scene, dusting through the room, searching every doorknob, dresser, table, handle— anything that could potentially reveal a print. Nothing was found. Not even in the bathroom where Richard had washed Jennie's blood away in the sink. Lastly, the window was checked. In the bright California sun, the screen was dusted. Sure enough, three solid prints along with a fourth smudged one were found. It was a step forward, a possible clue. They would need a suspect first, before they could compare the prints.

At 11 a.m. the following day, the autopsy was completed. All that the results established was that Jennie Vincow's murderer, was an experienced killer and a good one at that.

The murder of Jennie Vincow changed Richard. He needed to chase that high. He dove deeper into his cocaine addiction. Soon, Richard had to break into two to three homes a day to afford enough for cocaine. Always donned in all black, he slipped in and out of homes without a trace. Self-care was low on his list. He isolated himself, staying in his room, shooting cocaine, binge-watching MTV, and jamming out to loud heavy metal.

Several months passed. He hadn't suffered any repercussions from the murder or the countless break-ins. It was proof Satan was with Richard, like his dark guardian angel, granting permission to conceive these ideas and acts, then perform them.

One evening, Richard hopped into the driver's seat of a stolen car. The cocaine rushed through his system. He drove fast down the road, blasting his music. At some point, Richard lost control in the frenzied state and crashed the car into an LA bus station. He spent some time in jail after the incident and realized he no longer wanted to be some washed-up junkie from Skid Row. Cocaine made Richard slip up. He lost control, and if he wanted to kill more, there was no room for error. Richard renounced hard drugs, only smoking pot and drinking on occasion.

There was no high like killing.

On March 17, 1985, Richard arrived at the bus terminal in LA with one purpose: to purchase a .22 rifle. He described his weapon of choice fondly. "The bullet enters the skull and zigzags about without exiting, causing havoc to the brain; it's almost always fatal." After he retrieved the gun, he walked to a nearby gas station and stole a car while the owner was inside paying for gas. On the highway, he listened to *Highway to Hell* over and over again. Richard was going to murder tonight.

His eyes danced along the San Bernardino Freeway until they set upon a golden Camaro. Its driver was Maria Hernandez. She was young and beautiful, with shining eyes and olive skin. She'd just left dinner at her boyfriend's home and was returning for the evening in the suburb of Rosemead. Richard was locked onto his selected target.

He followed close behind for three blocks until she arrived at the condominium she shared with her roommate, Dayle Okazaki. Dayle had spent the day with her parents. Her family was very close and loving. She'd recently received a promotion to traffic supervisor with Los Angeles County. She'd worked hard to save up for the condo she now she shared with Maria. Like her roommate, she was very pretty, with shoulder-length hair and full lips.

She might have heard the garage door open as Maria parked her car. When Maria got out of her car, she was unaware that a killer had parked outside the condo on the street, and was now approaching her. The only thing with him was the .22 pistol gripped tightly in his palm. Maria moved to the door leading into the condo. She shuffled past the two parked cars and reached for the garage door opener. It groaned as the mechanisms worked to shut. She began to unlock the first of the two locks, her back facing away from Richard, who'd just bent down to slide beneath the shutting door. His AC/DC baseball cap fell to the concrete floor with his motion. He raised the pistol.

Perhaps she heard the sound of his footsteps or the falling of his hat, but Maria turned around to be face to face with Richard Ramirez. Twenty feet away, he walked toward her. She stared right down the barrel of his gun. His eyes were cold and dark he continued pressing forward.

"No, God, please don't! No!" she screamed, raising her hands over her face, which still clutched the keys to her golden Camaro. The gun was only twenty-four inches from her face, and as the garage door shut, total darkness enveloped them both.

Richard fired.

But miraculously, the bullet hit her car keys and deflected. Maria collapsed, lying on her side. She played dead. But an intense, stinging pain came from her hand. Fighting back the fear that caused her to tremble, she remained as still as possible.

Richard continued forward with his murdering spree, completely unaware that Maria was in fact unharmed. He kicked her out of the way and continued inside.

Dayle Okazaki was upstairs in the kitchen. She'd heard the shouts and the gunshot. The killer clad in all black entered, and in a frantic state of fear, Dayle ducked behind the kitchen counter where a vase held several flowers. She hoped that he hadn't spotted her.

But Richard had, and he was willing to wait. Slowing his breath, he stood in the doorway. He knew his prey would eventually have to come out. Shaking and confused, Dayle waited. Richard raised his gun, aiming where he knew she would rise.

In the garage, Maria hoisted herself off the cold, hard floor. She blinked, unsure what stroke of luck had saved her just then. She was still in shock. Opening the garage door, she took off running down the alley, unsure of what to do. Maria was scared and confused, running toward the front of the complex.

Several seconds passed inside. Unable to withstand the curiosity and confusion any longer, Dayle slowly pulled herself up, shaking with fear, hoping the intruder had left. She was unable to utter a single word or sentence, as her head passed the counter. Richard fired the gun. The bullet passed through Dayle's forehead, from which blood poured out. She fell back onto the floor, dead.

Richard left then, out the front door. He saw the figure of Maria hurrying down the sidewalk. He raised his gun. Their eyes locked. "Oh, please don't! Please don't kill me! Please don't shoot

85

me again!" She hid behind a Volkswagen. Richard was shocked to see her still alive. He had shot her point-blank a moment ago. Much to Maria's wonder, he did not shoot—instead, he hurried to where he'd parked his stolen car and jetted off, leaving behind his AC/DC hat as well as his first living witness.

Maria made her way back to the condominium after she'd watched the car and killer turn away. Her thoughts raced, and her mind was a complete jumble. Blood dripped from her hand, which seared with sharp pain. She waited to ensure the killer was long gone; then she hurried, stumbling. Dayle had been home and the killer inside. She had to get back.

She found her roommate in a pool of blood. Tears ran down her face as she called out Dayle's name, shaking her limp shoulder violently. Dayle didn't move. Maria raced through the house to make sure they were finally alone and then called the police.

Like a junkie who craves his high over and over, Ramirez wasn't finished as he drove along the freeway. Within the hour after Dayle's murder, his focus caught onto Veronica Yu, who was also driving along. She took the exit for Monterey Park. Veronica had spent the day grabbing lunch and chatting with a friend. She was tired and ready to relax at home, where she lived with her parents. She and her family had come to America from Taiwan.

Unlike Maria, Veronica noticed the Toyota trailing close behind her. She began searching for a cop car. About another block down, she decided to pull over and get a good look at the man stalking her. Richard noticed and decided to pass her up. He'd find someone else. But Veronica would follow him now.

On North Alhambra Avenue, a red light brought Richard to a stop. He got out of his car, turning the lights off. His gun was tucked beneath the waistband of his pants. His leather jacket shined in the red stoplight. Veronica rolled down her car window at his approach and demanded to know why Richard was following her.

"I'm not following. I thought I knew you," he responded. It wasn't good enough. She demanded again to know why! "I wasn't. I thought I knew you," he repeated himself.

"Liar," she snapped finally, backing her car up slowly. She told Richard she was going to call the police, memorizing the plate number of the Toyota.

Richard approached closer to the unrolled window. "I'm telling you, I thought I knew you. I wasn't following you—" he was egging her on, keeping her from driving away. When he was finally close enough, his hand thrust through the window like a snake striking a mouse and latched onto her shoulder. She screamed as he attempted to yank her through the window, twisting under his grasp.

It was no use. The driver's door was locked shut. He couldn't yank her out. But the passenger door was unlocked. He seized the opportunity, vaulting over the hood of the car. He was too fast. Veronica reached for the lock, but Richard was sitting beside her before she could press it down.

She pleaded with the man in black, wanting to know why he was doing this. In response, Richard shot her with his .22, below her right arm, seventeen inches from her head. Veronica screamed in pain and scrambled out of her car. Richard shot her once more. The bullet landed in her lower back. She wobbled for a bit as the pain took over, losing a shoe. She traveled several feet before falling onto the hard pavement, bleeding out.

"Help me! Help me! Help!" she cried out in agony. Ramirez gave her one last look over.

"Bitch," he called after her coldly, laughing as he returned to his Toyota, speeding away.

Richard drove off of the freeway, dumping the stolen Toyota. He hopped on the bus and returned to downtown LA like a soldier in Satan's army returning home after a long battle.

Unbeknownst to him, Jorge Gallegos had been sitting in a white pick-up truck with his girlfriend Edith Alcaaz. They'd watched Richard shoot Veronica. At first, they had figured it was nothing more than a lover's quarrel, but then they heard Veronica crying for help. Gallegos was the first to reach her as she breathed shallowly, still on the pavement. Edith's cousin, Joseph, who was in a nearby building on the second floor, heard the screams and had already called the cops when he witnessed Ramirez try to pull Veronica out of her car.

People gathered from the homes around Veronica as she lived her last few moments. She stopped breathing while talking to the police about what happened. After being rushed to the hospital, Veronica was officially pronounced dead; they were unsuccessful in reviving her. The witnesses were interviewed and their statements recorded.

For Dep. Gil Carrillo of Los Angeles Sheriff's Homicide ,that Sunday had been spent relaxing at home with his wife and three children. But the news of the Hernadez Okazaki attack came in, and Gil was out the door.

The clock was nearing midnight when Gil Carrillo arrived at the condo. He was quickly briefed on Maria's account and informed that she was at the hospital seeking treatment. He retraced the killer's path, immediately noticing the AC/DC hat on the garage floor. He walked through the scene of the crime, taking in the sight of it all. The first conclusion Gil came to was that some sort of love triangle was going on. Nothing had been stolen, so burglary was ruled out.

He would just need to speak to Maria.

The next afternoon, he visited her, finding Maria resting in a hospital bed. For someone standing at six-foot-four, Gil's kind and gentle demeanor contrasted his strong, massive build. He sat in the room beside her and listened to her describe the nightmarish experience. Maria had no idea who the man was nor what he would want from them. She and Dayle had a solid friendship—no secret lovers or estranged boyfriends.

She described the killer to Gil. "He was five-ten, thin, with black hair and dark, real scary eyes. I was opening the door to the house when I heard a noise, like maybe his foot on the ground. I turned and there he was, walking straight toward me." She agreed to help create a composite sketch, and Gil thanked her for her time. He left feeling more confused. What was the point of the murder?

After the autopsies of Veronica Yu and Dayle Okazaki, ballistics reported without complete certainty that the bullets used on both murders "most likely" came from the same gun. The bullet found in Dayle was too shattered for a 100-percent guarantee. Gil decided to call in for the advice of a legend in Los Angeles Law Enforcement, Frank Salerno.

In Gil's gut, he knew that this was the start of a murderous rampage.

Shut Up, Bitch

Richard Ramirez decided to live a life fully committed to murder—to domination and control. For Satan, he would rape and kill. He would please his new god. The darker and more vile the act, the more pleased Satan would be. After the three murders, Richard tailored his self-image. He made plans to steal enough to buy a home where he could set up a torture room. There, in privacy, he could kill and perform whatever Satanic ritual his heart desired. Perhaps he would even film the acts to sell on the black market. He knew there would be interest and potential buyers.

Ten days had passed since the double homicide. The police doubled down and tried everything they could to catch this killer before he struck again. They used street informants, checking up on leads and strange faces. But there simply wasn't enough to go off of.

On March 26, Richard hit the road once more to commit what could be considered one of his most savage murders. He had no planned destination, only the urge to kill. He passed by unsuspecting cars in the night when a sudden thought came to him. A year prior, Richard had robbed a home in Whittier. He recalled the wealth of the home—Whittier was a high-end area. That was where he would hit that night.

It was 2 a.m. when Richard returned to the home of Vincent and Maxine Zazzara. Richard remembered it well. It was a one-story, white ranch with two large bay windows. Fruit trees grew around the home. A light was on in the left window. He shut off the engine. He closed the car door without making a sound and approached the house like a deadly shadow.

Richard peered in through the window. His heart raced with excitement and danger. Vincent Zazzara was fast asleep on the couch. He had dozed off while watching television.

Richard slinked around the home to the backyard. From one of the back windows, he looked into the bedroom, where he caught the shape of forty-four-year-old Maxine. Watching a woman like this, knowing what he planned to do to her, caused arousal to course through Richard. He began to fumble with the screens, but the windows were closed and locked. He examined the home, searching for a potential point of entry and finally spotting one. He hoisted himself up toward a smaller window and removed the screen, prying the window open.

He entered the small laundry room. Carefully, he untied his shoes, setting them to the side. Richard made no sound as he approached the sleeping Vincent, the .22 pressed in his palm. Taking the combat position cousin Mike had taught him, he rushed in. With careful aim, he shot Vincent Zazzara in the left side of his head, right above the ear.

Vincent's eyes snapped open. His body went into shock. Disoriented and in pain, he attempted to rise from the couch and attack the man in all black. But the tiny bullet had done its damage. Vincent had lost control of his motor skills. Blood shot out from his wound, splattering on the wall.

The sound of the gunshot tore Maxine from her sleep. She snapped up out of bed. In horror and confusion, she screamed as the killer raced into her bedroom, the barrel of his gun directly aimed at her. "Shut up, bitch! And don't look at me. Where's the money? Where's the jewelry?" Richard shouted at her. Before he disconnected the phones, he forced her onto her stomach, binding then gagging her. He began to ransack the room, hungry for diamonds, gold, or cash.

Maxine knew about the shotgun kept under her bed. Vincent had purchased it, promising to shoot the thief who had visited them the year before. While Richard tore through their belongings, too engrossed to notice, Maxine managed to free herself from her bindings and reach underneath the bed to grab a hold of the shotgun. She rose and aimed the gun at the sweat-covered, agitated intruder.

Richard heard the noise and whipped around to see the shotgun pointed at him.

He began to reach for the gun in his own waistband.

Without wasting another second, Maxine shot the gun. Fury and anger tore through Richard. To Maxine's horror, only the sound of a metal click came out. Unbeknownst to her, her husband, who lay in the living room taking his last breath had, emptied the shotgun recently when their grandchildren had come to visit that weekend.

"Bitch! Motherfucker!" Richard screamed. The near-death experience threw him into a ballistic rage. He shot Maxine three times over, sending her backward and down. Richard beat her savagely, kicking and slapping her around. He couldn't believe she would attempt to shoot him—kill *him*! How dare she?

His blood boiled and adrenaline surged in his system. He rampaged to the kitchen and seized a ten-inch carving knife. Returning to the bedroom, knife in hand, Richard threw Maxine onto the bed and lifted her purple nightshirt up. Fueled by hate and rage, he began a futile attempt to carve Maxine's heart out. But he couldn't get through her rib cage and so settled on carving an upside-down cross into her chest over her left breast.

Her eyes would be the prize—he'd own then. First he cut away her eyelids with care, then removed her eyeballs, placing them in a little jewelry box he'd found that night. Richard laughed through it all. He stabbed her in a last rush of fury—in the stomach, pubic area, and throat. He attempted to have sex with her lifeless body, but the shock of the gun having been aimed at him had left Richard shaken.

He departed the home with a bundle of valuables in his arms, and his clothing stained in blood. Returning to the car, he kept the shot gun between his legs and carefully set the jewelry box with Maxine's eyes on the passenger seat.

He'd stuck a bumper sticker on the back of his car. "America, love it or leave it." He knew most cops were patriotic and thought perhaps it would help him evade being pulled over. Tonight, perhaps it worked. As Richard drove away, he noticed a police car trailing behind him. But he was never stopped. He made it all the way to his hotel room.

Richard washed the blood away from his clothes and changed. He then met with his main fence to sell the stolen valuables and guns from the Zazzaras. He pocketed the quick cash and made his way to pick up a prostitute. They settled on a quiet area to park and have sex, but Richard couldn't get an erection. He instead asked to play with the woman's feet. After, he drove the car down to Hollywood, where he abandoned it and took a bus back, walking along the urine-stained streets until the sun began to break along the horizon. He returned to his room at the seedy Cecil Hotel on Main and opened the jewelry box. He examined Maxine's eyes and laughed gleefully.

The officers arrived two days later, shocked by the grisly murders. The sight of Maxine Zazzara's mutilated face horrified even the most seasoned of detectives. The autopsy revealed the bullets had been enough to kill Maxine. The stabbing and mutilation had been nothing more than an act of pleasure for the killer. One officer later recalled the scene: "The eyes were missing. There were ... little indentations ... and scratch marks around the eyes. It was very bloody, a lot of blood and disfigurement. I hope I never live to see anything like it again."

They scoured the home for fingerprints, but Richard hadn't left one behind. He'd been too careful, too skilled. Except he'd overlooked one significant detail: his shoes. Richard Ramirez wore Avia Aerobic sneakers. The police found his size 11-1/2 foot in the flower bed beneath the window. At the time, only 1,354 pairs of Avia Aerobic sneakers had been made, and only six pairs actually sold in L.A.

Another clue.

Upon hearing the news of the Zazzara murders, a gut instinct told Carillo this was his man. These tragic murders were all linked to one single person. Whether or not the other officers believed him, he knew it was true.

On April 14, Richard made his way to Cameo Theater on Broadway, a joint pressed to his lips. Here, he could watch pornos twenty-four seven. Richard then made his way to a pool hall, to hit a few balls around. He'd had a fairly normal day, but behind those eyes another dark, twisted plan was brewing.

Early that week, Richard had picked up a police scanner at a RadioShack. He had it with him as he hopped into a car that he stole from in front of Alexandria Hotel. He had to be smarter, stay ahead of the police. Richard's dream was to be one of the best serial killers in history. AC/DC's *Highway to Hell* album blasted. The hunt began once more for the kill. He drove along the freeway, once again getting off at the Monterey Park exit. He parked the car on Trumbower Avenue. The night was late and the sky black, matching Richard's uniform of murder. He stopped the engine of the car, flicking its lights off. Most of the resident's cars were pulled into the garage, out of the streets. They would be sleeping peacefully now in the silent night that masked Richard.

He slipped out of the car, sticking close to the cloak of shadows, and walked south along the street. He stopped outside the home of William and Lilian Doi. At sixty-six years old, William was retired. The day prior, he'd finalized the down payment on a brand new Ford Van. He and Lilian made plans to travel through America with one another. Fifty-six years old, Lilian had suffered from a debilitating stroke two years ago. It had taken much of her ability to talk, and her mobility was limited to a wheelchair. Still, she was just as eager as her husband for the upcoming trip.

It had begun to rain a light drizzle over Richard when he decided on his target. He headed for the backyard first. His feet moved with a quick and deliberate pace. The drops of rain masked his sound, kept the people at home and off the road. Richard first noticed the alarms and wires around the windows. He settled on one that was already opened—all he needed to do was slice through the screen and slip into the home. He entered into the rear bathroom, all the while repeating his mantra: "Satan, this, what I, your humble servant, am about to do, I do for you."

Laying low, he let the moment of his initial arrival pass, and then quiet as a mouse he moved into the hall. A light was on, and his eyes adjusted. He could see easily now, and through the open doorway, he caught a glimpse of Lillian Doi, who was fast asleep. He took note of her wheelchair in the bedroom.

He continued to the room of William Doi. Due to Lillian's condition, they slept separately. Richard raised his silver-plated .22 automatic. It was new and recently purchased, replacing his revolver. There was no hiding the hard metal click of the gun as Richard chambered it. William's eyes snapped open. He recognized the sound immediately and carefully opened the drawer of his nightstand and pulled out a 9-millimeter pistol. Richard saw Doi attempt to grab his gun.

Ricard shot him, standing in the combat position. The bullet traveled through William's head, above his upper lip and through his tongue. It lodged in the back of Bill's throat. He choked, gagging on it, falling from his bed. Richard attempted to fire his gun again, but this time the bullet became lodged. He swore and cleared the gun out in the hall.

Bill tried to plead with the killer dressed in all black. The bullet had done its damage to his voice box, brain, and mouth. He was losing a profuse amount of blood, and was unable to make out any sentences or words.

Lillian had heard the gun and the cries of her husband, desperately pleading, unable to articulate. She could not move, only lie in bed and listen to the horror unfurling in the room next door.

Richard released a fury of blows with his massive fists down onto Bill, knocking the poor man unconscious. Richard then made his way into Lillian's room. He slapped her hard, warning her not to scream. "Shut up, or I'll kill you, bitch," Richard told her. Even if Lillian had wanted to cry for help, she would have be unable to. Her stroke had taken much of her verbal ability away.

Richard used thumb cuffs to bind Lillian's arms behind her back, then went to town on the home, rifling through everything. Lillian listened as the intruder opened drawers and ripped through dressers, spilling items everywhere.

All the while, Bill regained consciousness. His head pounded and the pain bolted through him. Blood dripped down his mouth from the wound. Richard noticed him rising and ran back, knocking Bill out once more. The violence of it all excited Richard greatly. He felt alive, charged, and sexually aroused. He returned to Lillian's bedroom and raped her. He relished in the fear and panic that overtook her. He'd completely dominated her, telling her not to look at him. Richard finished by kissing Lillian, then stuffed his new stolen goodies in two pillowcases, disabled one of the two phones, and left the home leaving Lillian bound by the thumb cuffs.

All the while, Bill lay on the floor. The pain was overtaking him, but he fought to come to. The man in all black was gone, but his wife was still there and he worried greatly for her. He could hear her cries and moans. With blood pouring from his mouth, Bill crawled to his wife's room. He saw her then, lying on the bed, her hands bound. With every last bit of strength, Bill made it to the second phone.

It was around 5 a.m. when the dispatcher received the call. Darlene Boese, a dispatcher for the Monterey Park Police Department, answered.

"I asked if he needed an ambulance, but he couldn't do anything except choke or gurgle."

"Help," he barely managed to speak to the emergency dispatcher before passing out. Then Bill regained consciousness, and called 911 once more. "Help me," he managed a second time. Darlene Boese reassured him help was well on its way.

Tears fell from Lillian's eyes as she struggled to free herself from the thumb cuffs. She managed to pull her right hand free, slicing her thumb. It took all her strength, but she only managed to make it to the doorway of the hall. The firefighter met her there. He later described finding her. She "was in her nightgown. She had a pair of thumb cuffs on her left thumb ... her face was swollen and there was bluing around her mouth and chin area. She wasn't speaking." At first it seemed as though she didn't understand, but she pointed to her husband, who sat in his chair, unconscious. Blood ran down his face, staining his shirt. Each of his breaths was extremely labored and slow. They attempted to perform CPR, clearing out a space on the floor.

Richard had left a tornado of a mess in his wake. Bill was rushed away to the hospital.

One of the officers stayed behind to speak with Lillian, but between her stroke and the shock of the night, she had a difficult time communicating with the officers. Still, she managed to let them know it was a tall man donned in all black with a gun and horrible, rotting teeth. She and her husband had no known enemies. The only clear motive was burglary as the house was completely trashed. They took her to the hospital soon after her husband.

At 5:29 am, Bill Doi died in the ambulance. His last act alive had been to call 911 for his wife.

After the attack on the Dois, Richard Ramirez's spree would hit one after the other in quick succession.

The night of May 29, around 11:30 p.m., Richard found his next target. Mabel Bell was eighty-three years old and lived with her younger sister Florence "Nettie" Lang, eighty-one. Their home was located about twenty miles northeast of Los Angeles. Mabel Bell was an active senior. She went out and played Bridge three nights a week. Her husband had passed away early on in their marriage, but she managed to raise her two children on her own and have twelve grandchildren. She took in her sister, who had several health issues, so Nettie wouldn't have to be institutionalized.

As for Richard, he drove with no map. He used his instincts to guide him down the road. Mabel Bell's residence was the first he came to. He stopped the car, enveloping himself in the silence he knew and loved so well. There wasn't another home for a half mile or so. He got out then, careful not to make a sound when he shut the car door.

Flashlight in hand, he was happy to see that the front door was not locked. The older women didn't worry about crime. But anger filled him when he realized there was little to steal. These elderly women had nothing of value. He found a hammer and returned to Nettie's bedroom. He repeatedly beat her head with it. He grabbed the electric cord from the alarm clock on her bedside table and tied her hands behind her back. The clock stopped six minutes after midnight, falling to the floor. Richard left then, not realizing he'd stepped on the clock and left a bloody footprint in it.

Mabel Bell was awakened by the hammer crashing down on the side of her head. She screamed, thinking perhaps it was a terrible nightmare, but it was not. Richard called upon Satan as he beat her

105

savagely. "Shut up or I'll kill you! Where's the money? Where's the jewelry?" he screamed at her. Pieces of her brain splattered against the wall as his hammer came down time and time again. He flipped on the lights and used duct tape to bind her ankles. Then, with the use of the electric cord he ripped from her clock, he shocked her. Mabel Bell was half-conscious as the bolts of electricity tore through her beaten, tired body. He scrambled to steal whatever he could find, including the cassette player Mabel's grandson had bought that year for her birthday. It was her first one.

The violence of everything caused Richard's blood to rush through him. His dark sexuality pulsed with desire. He returned to Nettie's room and ripped her nightgown from her, raping her violently. He found a tube of Mabel's red lipstick. With it, he left a pentagram upon Mabel's thigh as well as on the white wall above her still body. He drew another in Nettie's bedroom on the wall for the police to find.

He took his time after to bask in the quiet home of his savage escapade, devouring a banana and drinking a can of coke and mountain dew. His work was done, and with the blood-stained

106

pillowcase pressed in his arms, he left, driving home in a solo parade for Satan.

The night at Mabel Bell's had left Richard charged. He needed another release immediately or else he would implode. Each fiber in his being was desperate for another kill. The very next evening he hit the road once more, dressed in his hellish uniform for murder. He arrived on the sleeping streets of Burbank. Here, there was more money, more for him to take. He was equipped that night with his set of cuffs and a .25 automatic, as well as his .22 auto. Earlier that day, he'd found several stacks of books and put them in the backseat of his car. That way, if the police tried to shoot him from behind, the bullets would be stopped. He'd seen it in a movie once.

He stopped outside a beige home in Burbank. All the windows and doors were locked, but Richard found a puppy door. He bent down on his hands and knees and reached up through it. He found the lock, and with his deft fingers he unlocked the door, stepping through with ease. It couldn't have been any easier for Richard. He clicked on the penlight. His .22 was drawn close and ready.

He first came across the bedroom of forty-two-year-old Carol Kyle. He hovered over her bed. But she was alone, and Richard had to ensure he took care of any potential threats looming in the homestead. He pressed the cold, hard metal of his gun to the side of her head. The bright beam from the penlight blinded her. "Wake up, bitch! And don't scream, or I'll kill you. Don't make a fucking sound! Understand?"

"I understand," she said. Her mind scrambled, still foggy from sleep. He demanded to know who else was in the house. She told him the only other person was her eleven-year-old son, Mark. Richard demanded to be shown the boy.

Carol remained as calm as she could. Her son's life depended on it. She was a nurse and had experienced myriad emergencies. She knew how to keep composure, handle stress—she'd be able to handle this psycho. Carol led Richard to her son's room, but Richard had learned the hard way that these people might try to pull a gun on him. He instructed her to lie down with her head on the ground and not make sound or he would kill her.

Then in one quick movement, Richard barreled into the eleven-year-old's room, pressing the gun against Carol's son's head.

"Don't fuckin' move. Don't look at me, and don't move!" Richard snapped. Carol lurched from the floor, throwing herself between the killer and her son. "Please don't hurt him. Take whatever you want, just don't hurt him, please!" she begged. Her only goal was to protect her son, and she would see it through. Richard demanded Carol not look at him. He handcuffed the two of them together ,then threw them in a closet. Then, on second thought, he opened the closet back up and asked if they owned any guns. Carol told him there were no guns in their house. Richard didn't believe her. Instead, he ripped them out of the closet and had them lie face down in Carol's bedroom with a sheet pulled over them. He began his process of tearing apart the home, searching and swearing at Carol.

He then moved them back to the closet and continued his ransacking. Carol remained calm for her son. She reassured him that it was all going to be okay. She wouldn't let her son see an ounce of panic on her face.

After Richard finished his search, he returned to the closet and uncuffed Carol from her son. Then he cuffed Mark's hands behind his back and left him in the closet, so Richard could drag Carol by her hair back to her bedroom.

Upon finding out that Carol had a sixteen-year-old daughter, he laughed when he threatened to wait for her to return home from a friend's house. To Carol, it sounded like the high-pitched cackling of a dog. She was prepared to take whatever this horrible man decided to throw at her, but she knew her daughter couldn't. Again he repeated his demands for her. "And don't fuckin' look at me, bitch!" He had to keep his identity hidden. Her eyes stayed down, and she led him to the dresser where she kept her jewelry.

With reluctance, she gave him the diamond she wore around her neck on a thin gold chain. It had come off her wedding ring, which she'd turned into a necklace after her husband had been killed. He snatched it from her hands, then bound them behind her back with panty hose, covering her head with a pillow on the bed.

"All right, where's the other diamonds? And where's the cash, bitch?" he asked. She let him know there was nothing else hidden. She had very little after her husband passed away. Carol promised, begging Richard not to hurt her son.

"Don't worry, you do what I say and you'll both be all right," he said as he ripped the nightgown from her body and forced her to perform oral sex on him. Carol knew resistance was not an option. This man would kill her without hesitation. She saw it. She described it to the police. "The look in his eyes was absolutely demonic. Never had I seen eyes like his on a human being."

He flipped her over and began to sodomize her. When he was done, he once again scoured through the home, frantically searching for any valuables that he may have missed. His motions were frantic, and he moved haphazardly, as though nervous. Carol worried. He seemed to be on edge, ready to snap at any second. His edginess translated to sexual energy. He wasn't satisfied, not yet. He sodomized her again. Carol begged him to stop. But her pleas only increased his pleasure.

Sweat ran down his skin. He moved to the kitchen to get a glass of water.

Finally, dawn began to creep along the edge of the horizon. Ramirez asked Carol for directions to the highway. He seemed confused and turned around.

"You must have had a very bad life to do this to me," she finally said to Richard.

"You're lucky I'm letting you live. I've killed a lot of people, you know." He laughed once more as a thought passed through his twisted mind. "I'm going to bring your son in here—"

She begged Richard to not let her son see her naked.

Much to Carol's surprise, Richard gave her a nightgown to put on. Warning her not to look at him, or else he'd cut her eyes out, Richard brought her son, Mark, out of the closet, and the two of them were handcuffed to the headboard of the bed. Then, before leaving, he put the handcuff key on the mantel, letting Carol know it was for her daughter to use when she came home.

He left then. Stuck to the bed, Carol waited with her son in the silence of their home, as the engine of Richard's car starting came from outside. Mark reached the phone, and he dialed 911.

At 6:05 a.m., an officer arrived at Carol's home to catch Mark's small hand waving out the bedroom window. Carol helped create a composite sketch.

Forty-eight hours had passed since Richard had attacked Mabel Bell and Nettie Lang. Their bodies remained still and undiscovered. At seventy-eight years old, Carlos Valenzuela worked as a gardener and handyman in the local area. He'd known Bell for twenty-four years and helped care for her yard and pool. After a day, he passed by the home a second time and noticed several newspapers left alone on the stairs. He figured the two sisters might have fallen ill, so he entered the home, calling out for both of them. There was Nettie, half-alive, her eyes wide open. Blood caked and dried. A pentagram drawn overhead upon the wall. Everything had been upturned and thrown about. The remnants of a banana were set on the table. He bolted from the home, praying. Quickly, he drove to the closest home, and together they called the police.

The sisters were rushed to the hospital. Both were in comatose states.

As the police began their investigation through the home, none knew exactly what the pentagram meant except that whoever did this was most likely a follower of Satan. Upon hearing about the attack, Gil Carillo was unsure if this was linked to the other murders. If that was the case, then they were dealing with a murderer who had no profile, no type. He just killed for the sake of it.

Anyone could be his victim. And so the fear began.

Night Stalker

It didn't take long until Richard was ready for another kill. In a stolen Toyota, he made his way to Pico Rivera. His eyes scanned, and he settled on the home of John Rodriguez and his wife, Susan. But unfortunately for Richard, John was a sheriff. He slept with his revolver on his bedside table. He'd gone off to bed, and Susan dozed off on the sofa in the living room while watching the late night news.

Outside, Richard moved in silence, cloaked in the layer of darkness. To his dismay, all the windows and doors he tried were locked. Finally, on the side of the house, he came across an unlocked window leading into the dining room. It was sealed shut with paint, but Richard picked away at the layer with a screwdriver and pried it loose. He began to slide it open, but he stopped. Frozen. His heart raced. Sweat ran down his skin as his blood coursed through his veins.

Susan called out to her husband, asking if he'd opened the window. John Rodriguez assured her he had not. That window had been sealed shut since they'd painted the dining room two years ago.

Now, the break-in was far too great of a risk. Richard backed away and returned to his car. Tonight would not be his.

At home, Gil Carillo received a phone call. An officer had found an Avia foot print in Pico Rivera after an attempted break-in at one of the deputy's homes.

Being so close, so charged to exercise his wrath and murder, Richard was furious and hungry for more. Even as the light of the sun began to rise, Richard was eager for a kill. In Eagle Rock, he attempted to snatch a young girl from the street, but she was tough. Her screams and fighting let her escape his grasp and run away. A ground floor resident in a nearby building heard the girl's cries and quickly dialed 911.

Richard drove off in a hurry. He headed for the highway, only to be stopped when bright red lights flashed behind him. LAPD motorcycle officer John Stavros pulled him over. From his car window, Richard pitched his weed as well as a gun before he obliged, stopping the car.

Stavros asked for the license and registration. Richard did his best to tell the officer that he'd left his wallet at home. In response, Stavros asked Richard to step out of the vehicle and place his hands on the hood of the car. He searched Richard, but found nothing. The officer asked for a name, and in the end decided to let the killer go with nothing more than a ticket.

Richard gave a fake name and a random downtown address. Stavros returned to his motorcycle to write the ticket, but as he did, he overheard on the radio about the attempted abduction of the little girl in Eagle Rock. "Mexican, black hair, driving a blue Toyota."

Richard knew, even if the officer was completely unaware. He would have to leave—soon. Officer Stavros returned after writing up the ticket.

"Hey … you're not that guy killing people in their homes, are you?" he asked.

"No way man; when are you guys going to catch that motherfucker?"

"We'll get him."

"Hope so. I got a wife, you know."

"You sure you're not him?"

"Hey man, it's not me, c'mon here."

Officer Stavros made his way back to his motorcycle. Richard quickly prayed to Satan. He drew a pentagram on the hood of the car and dashed away from the officer. Stavros hopped on his motorcycle

116

and tried to chase after, but Richard had already leaped over a ten foot fence and was long gone.

The police were hard at work to catch the suspected killer. Gil Carillo and Frank Salerno officially partnered up. Gil's normal partner was on vacation, and Frank's was in the hospital for surgery. It was time for them to work together and stop the killer in black.

The night they teamed up, they celebrated at a Chinese restaurant. And the next day, they were called in for a homicide.

Patty Elaine Higgins of Arcadia was only twenty-eight years old. She was kind and easygoing, with light blonde hair. She was a teacher at the Braddocks School. That day, she'd helped the foreman from the construction site across her street run on an extension of her phone line. She told him it was fine.

While Gil Carillo and Frank Salerno had been out celebrating their partnership, Richard Ramirez was making a stop at Patty's home. Dressed in all black, he approached the back door of the building. He broke the window pane and slunk in like a shadow.

With no one else home, Richard had his way with the young, attractive school teacher. He aggressively sodomized her, while she was bent over on her hands and knees in the bathroom. He ransacked her home, beating Patty with no mercy, and when he was finished, Richard sliced her throat so deeply, he nearly decapitated her.

This was the scene he left for Gil and Frank to find the next day. Both had the gut instinct telling them this was their guy, except there was no shoe print and no gun used in the attack. There was nothing, not even a finger print.

Richard had no clue the evidence was being gathered as the police hunted for the killer. Several other crimes popped up and the authorities began to link this "Valley Intruder" to them. A nine-year-old boy had been kidnapped from his home in Monterey Park, sodomized, and abandoned. Another young girl in Eagle Rock had been raped at gunpoint, after a man broke into the family's home while the parents slept. A teenager was babysitting when an intruder broke in and raped her.

It was July 2, and the heat was unbearable, suffocating everyone in L.A. with its wicked grasp. People were moving slowly. The city burned under the sun, but none of this deterred Richard.

He was like a demonic force, thriving in the fire of hell. Sweat ran down his brow as he walked along the streets of Arcadia. He'd returned, figuring the police wouldn't expect him back so soon. This time he stopped outside the home of seventy-five-year-old Mary Louise Cannon. He opened a window to the beige home, where the widow lived alone, and entered.

Mary had beaten cancer twice in her life. She was strong and didn't give up easily. Even in her later years, she wasn't afraid to live life, and had a trip to Australia with a group of seniors planned. Richard quickly gathered that Mary was the only one home. He searched through the rooms with a pen light, immediately triggered with rage and the need to murder. He lifted the lamp off of Mary's dresser and slammed it down on the side of her head.

The pain tore through Mary, and she awoke screaming. Richard savagely beat her with his fists. She was unconscious in a matter of seconds, and yet Richard continued to attack. He choked her, then hurried to find a knife.

A murderous frenzy of assault consumed Richard. Over and over, he sank the metal of the butcher's knife deep in Mary's throat. Blood gushed with each deadly stab.

When the thrill of murder had been satisfied, Richard stepped away from Mary, stealing whatever he could from her home. Drunk in the ecstasy Richard found in murder, he drove off in his stolen Toyota, heading right to his fence to sell the goods he'd just captured.

Frank and Gil arrived in the morning. The violent death of Mary matched too closely to that of Patty Higgins. It clicked then through the police department what Gil had been trying to say all along. All these twisted murders were being committed by the same killer. A footprint of the same size and general shape of the Avia shoes had been left on Mary's carpet. Salerno later described the collected evidence after that day. "The knife wound tied Patty and Mary together, and the shoe prints tied in the Zazzara killings and abduction cases." The investigators realized they had one of the most dangerous killers ever on their hands. He murdered at random, with no preferred weapon. He was wild and unpredictable, and that was what made him so deadly, so frightening.

The Avia footprint, the heinous breath, the smell of wet leather and the man dressed in all black. All of it was coming together to point toward Richard, who was not about to stop his killing. In his mind, the power of Satan protected him like a cloak from bitter winter. It did not matter how many police cruisers searched for him. The need to kill was far too good of a high for Richard to give up.

He returned to Arcadia on July 4, tuning into the police scanner. He listened, keeping track of where the police were looking. A call came about a prowler. It dawned on him then, that the police were looking for him. They referred to him as the "Valley Intruder." But he did not stop that night. Satan was with him.

He parked down Arno Drive, having picked a ranch with massive windows in the front. He discovered the backdoor was locked shut, but the front door was open and welcoming. Richard entered the home with his .22 automatic ready to fire. Mr. and Mrs. Steve Bennett were fast asleep along with their two children, Whitney and James.

The family had been out celebrating the Fourth of July. They'd had company over and usually used the back door. Their sixteen-year-old daughter Whitney had been at a party with friends. She'd come home late, and around 1:00 a.m., the cute teenager with chestnut hair and bright blue eyes had slipped into her pajamas and gone to bed.

Richard entered Whitney's bedroom first, where he found her fast asleep. His penlight scanned the room, and he immediately approached her dresser, taking her jewelry and watch. The young woman got him excited, but before Richard could have his way with her, he would need to secure any potential threats in the home.

Tonight, he decided he wouldn't use his gun. Instead, he returned to his car and pulled out a tire iron. He had big plans to bludgeon everyone to death.

He slipped through Whitney's opened window. The sight of her lying still and innocent aroused him. Excitement shot through him. Tonight he killed for Satan. His hand clamped tightly over her mouth and the tire iron came down upon her head. He beat her with it, then decided to switch to his knife. For Richard the act of stabbing was for more personal. It was like sex. He ventured to the kitchen to hunt for a knife, but came up empty handed. He returned to her bedroom. Crimson blood dripped off the tire iron.

He wanted to rape her then, but to prevent her cries from waking the household and alerting her father, Richard reasoned he'd have to kill her first. His eyes fell upon the telephone wire. He'd use that to strangle her.

With the wire in hand, Richard climbed on top of Whitney, straddling her. She lay on her stomach. Her head rang with fierce pain. Richard wrapped the wire around her neck and pulled. The fight for oxygen took over.

Richard froze in the midst of his murder.

Sparks shot from the wire. A blue haze emanated from Whitney's body as she lay beneath him. Fear crept through Richard. He thought he caught a glimpse of her soul. He released the wire.

Richard scampered away, scurrying out the window and returning to the car. He feared Christ himself had intervened and appeared to save the teenager's life.

To Richard, the incident with Whitney seemed a sign that his power and Satan's protection were weakening. But he was still wound up. It was close to morning then. He'd never consummated his sexual needs. He needed more—proof he was still in control, retaining his power.

He found a prostitute, who only laughed at him when he wanted to have sex with her feet. He threw her out of his car, anger surging. So he chose to return to his hotel room. Sleep did not come for him then. He lay awake, his thoughts racing.

It was almost 6 a.m. when Whitney came to. Her head screamed with agony. This was no normal headache. Shock and panic overcame her when she saw the blood-soaked sheets around her. She'd no memory of the attack. A hysterical scream rang from her as she leaedt from her bed, only to fall in the doorway. She cried out for her father.

123

Her parents found her then, shocked at the horrible sight. Their poor daughter's face was beaten and swollen. They held their daughter, consoling her, and dialed the police. When they asked her what happened, she repeated, "I don't know."

Frank Salerno was retiring for bed in the wee hours of the morning when he caught the call from Gil Carillo.

"Well, we got another one, partner. In Sierra Madre. A teenage girl's been beaten and left for dead in her parents' home. It's him, Frank. I know it."

Without missing a beat, Frank arrived at the Bennets' home. A tire iron had never been used by the Valley Intruder. But it was one of the bloodiest attacks Frank and Gil had seen. They knew it was their guy. Their gut instinct was only reaffirmed when a bloody footprint left on Whitney's comforter was identified as an Avia shoe.

Grandmother of five and a divorcee, Joyce Lucille Nelson awoke to Richard's .22 pressed against her head. It was July 7 and she'd fallen asleep on the couch with the television on. Joyce resisted Richard, and in a flurry of rage, he grabbed a fist full of her hair and dragged her to the bedroom. There Richard beat the elderly woman to death so savagely, he left the imprint of his Avia shoe perfectly embedded in her face.

But it wasn't enough. He continued driving, searching the streets. At 3 a.m., he parked on Hollywood Oak Drive. He settled on the home of sixty-three-year-old Sophie Dickman, using the doggy door to enter.

Fueled with rage and the thirst for more spilled blood, the follower of Satan found Sophie in her bed. He charged in without wasting a second. She awoke to his hand hooked over her mouth. Wild rage burned in his eyes like a twisting fire. In a growl, he told her, "Don't look at me! Don't make a fucking sound, or I'll kill you!" Sophie knew who this man was. She'd read about the intruder in the papers. He'd come to her home this time. Yet she remained calm and quiet. Years working as a psychiatric nurse helped her in that moment. He handcuffed her, throwing a pillowcase over her head and led her to the bathroom floor. There she waited, as Richard tore through her home and disconnected the phones.

After he made several demands, she brought him to the second bathroom and showed him where her valuable jewels were kept inside the medicine cabinet. Richard took it all, including her diamond ring, which she attempted to hide from him. He then yanked her into the bedroom and tore away her nightclothes.

He shoved a glove into her mouth, telling her to bite down on it, so she wouldn't scream. She obliged. Then he pulled a pillow over her face. She thought he planned to suffocate her, but instead he undid his zipper and attempted to rape her. However, Richard couldn't get an erection. He cursed and demanded she roll onto her stomach. Sophie did so, but Richard still failed in his attempt to sodomize her.

Sophie knew it was up to her to remain as calm as possible. She understood the nature of a psychopath. This killer needed to feel as though he were in control. She feared he may grow embarrassed and enraged with being unable to perform sexually and kill her. She knew he needed to dominate the situation completely. She couldn't incite any more of his temperamental anger. Anything could be a switch to cause Richard to flip right off.

Richard handcuffed her to the bed. This time, he successfully raped her, demanding to know where the other valuables were. When she told him there was nothing more, he made her swear to Satan there was nothing. She did, in a calm voice. He left her handcuffed to the bed then, with a pillowcase full of valuables, and immediately brought his night's bounty to his fence at the bus station. They agreed on a price and the sun rose into the morning sky.

When Sophie was sure the killer was long gone, she used every ounce of her strength to pull the bed to the nearest window. There she called out for her next door neighbor, a woman in law enforcement. The neighbor, woken from sleep, heard Sophie and hurriedly called the police.

As a living witness, Sophie described her assailant. He was tall and thin, but more notably his breath smelled and he was dressed in all black. Though this description matched all the others, law enforcement was not any closer to finding an identity.

Fear began to spread through the area. Sales of locks went up, as well as guard dogs. Lines were seen stretching out of gun stores. The media took hold of the story and the news of it all spread like wildfire.

And so Richard Ramirez was no longer known as the Valley Intruder. He became "the Night Stalker."

On July 17, Mabel Bell died from her brain injuries. Her sister Nettie survived.

Richard consumed everything published about him with great excitement. He lived for the fame and the news reporting on each of his murders.

On July 20, Richard decided to give the media the story that would blow up in the headlines. He purchased for his next murder an industrial machete. He had plans to shock everyone by decapitating his next victims and placing their heads in the front yard on display. He chose an area of Glendale and arrived at the home of the Kneidings. All the doors were secured and locked. The Kneidings had kept up on the news and were aware of the intruder. Richard decided to cut through the screen of a French door and easily undo the lock.

Before entering with the machete clutched tightly in his hands, Richard dropped down to one knee and said his prayer. "By all that is evil, I, your humble servant, invoke Satan to be here and accept this offering." Inside, Richard searched the home as always to find out who was around. It was only Max and Lela Kneiding. They were both in their sixties and had known each other for over fifty years. They were high school sweethearts, and between the two of them they had three grown children.

Richard turned on the light of the bedroom and woke them up with "Rise and shine, motherfuckers!" A scream came out of Lela as Richard swung the machete, slicing through Max's neck. Much to Richard's disappointment, the machete hadn't been sharp enough to remove their heads. Instead, Max dropped down to his knees with a giant gash left in his neck, pleading. Richard swung at Lela, but he missed. The killer grabbed his trusty .22. He pushed it against Max's head, pulling the trigger, but the gun jammed. They begged him not to shoot, but their pitiful pleas were nothing more than music to Richard's ears. He unjammed the gun and shot them both.

The chaos in the home fell into deathly silence. In the fiery passion of murder, Richard proceeded to stab and slash away at them with his machete. The police scanner he'd brought inside with him reported gunshots had been heard. Richard moved fast. He filled a pillowcase with stolen goods and dashed out of the home. Speeding to the freeway, he left the empty fog-covered streets of the suburbs.

Their bodies were found by their thirty-six-year-old daughter. Lela had been so badly beaten and ravaged her bones and vital organs were exposed. And Max's head was nearly decapitated. It was a savage butchery.

That very night, Richard drove straight to his fence, who immediately noticed all of the blood on him. If Richard was in fact the Night Stalker in the newspaper and radio, the fence knew it was best not to say a word. That would mean Richard was one of the deadliest men around. But it wouldn't take long until the fence stopped doing business with him.

Taking the cash from the Kneidings' stolen goods, Richard wasn't satisfied. Like the true junkie that he was, he wanted more. He drove to Sun Valley. It was a quarter after four in the morning. Sun Valley was north, away from all the killing and murder. And even though the people there knew about the Night Stalker, none dared think that they were within his range.

Chainarong and Somkid Khovananth were asleep at home with their two younger children; one was eight and the other two.

Fast asleep in the den, Somkid was jerked awake by the sudden movement in their home. A hand clamped down over her mouth. Richard's gun met the side of Somkid's head. He told her to not make a sound or else he would kill her. She nodded, and Richard made his way to the bedroom, where Chainarong snored loudly. The fan running in the bedroom offered little relief from the sweltering heat.

Inches from Chainarong's head, Richard fired the gun. A muffled shot sounded as the bullet tore through Chainarong's skull. He died instantly. Richard returned to Somkid in the den.

This was the process Richard came to use over and over. He'd take out the men in the house and rape the wives and daughters. It was a cowardly technique, and the police had taken note of it.

Riled up, Richard was anxious to rape and subject Somkid to his torture. He beat her savagely until blood poured from her nose and mouth. He tore off her nightgown, forced her up, and after retrieving a knife, had her lead him to the bathroom. There he cut the cord of a hair dryer and then brought her to the bedroom, where Somkid's dead husband lay. Fear took hold. Her terror excited Richard more as he raped her after using the cord to bind her. She did not fight back.

The alarm clock from the eight-year-old's room went off. Richard bolted into the child's room. He bound the child and shoved a sock into his mouth. Then he began to rifle through the room tearing it apart. He then forced Somkid out of the bedroom and into a chair, making her fellate him. Finally he reached climax by sodomizing her.

His hand grabbed a fistful of hair and he dragged her through the house, slapping her, cursing and kicking her, demanding to know

131

where the valuables were. First, she directed him to her purse, where he pocketed eighty dollars. Then, after several more threats, she told him about the stash of rare diamonds and jewelry they had.

"And where's the money?" he hissed.

"No money, no money! I swear, I swear to God!"

"No! Swear to Satan."

"I swear to Satan, no money! I swear to Satan. I swear to Satan!" She was still tied and naked, and Richard heaved her back into the bedroom to rape her again. There he left her. She watched in horror as he snatched a bottle of baby oil from the dresser and entered her young son's room. Somkid could do nothing but listen to her son's terrifying screams and several slaps.

After Richard beat Somkid and stole everything of value he could find, he exited the room. It is estimated he walked out with $30,000 of goods. Somkid waited, bound on the bedroom floor. He was gone. She quickly freed herself and ran to her son to ensure he was alright. She held her son, who was bleeding from his rectum. Then she pulled back the blanket of her husband and saw the bullet wound lodged in his head. She kept the painful emotions from taking over, holding her composure for her two children. With them both in her arms, she ran to the neighbors, crying and shouting for help.

The attack in Sun Valley wasn't immediately linked to the Night Stalker. It was too far north, even though Somkid described her attacker as "brown-skinned, bad teeth, thirty to thirty-five, 150 pounds, six-foot-one or so."

The fear and the panic spread. Richard Ramirez's murders were on the cover of every newspaper. Eldery women were afraid to be left alone. Calls came into the authorities in a constant stream of men dressed in all black. Patrols were added to neighborhoods. Enormous pressure fell upon the police, and the neighboring jurisdictions finally began to work together.

Richard was at the pinnacle of the fear he spread throughout. And nothing was going to stop him. In a freshly stolen Toyota, he arrived at the home of Virginia and Chris Petersen. They were a young couple and lived in their modest, but well maintained home with their five-year-old daughter. After poking and prodding around the outside of the house, Richard located an open sliding glass door. It led into the living room, where he slid inside. Richard knelt down upon his knee inside the dark, quiet home and silently prayed to Satan as a humble servant. The .25 automatic was secured in his grip.

Richard found Chris and Virginia fast asleep in their bed together. Virginia woke to the hard metal click of the gun, readying to fire. Her eyes snapped open and she locked onto the dark figure standing in her bedroom. "Who the hell are you, what do you want?" Virginia asked frantically. "Get out!"

A nasty laugh answered her.

"Shut up, bitch." With those cold words, Richard moved closer, firing the gun. The bullet seared through Virginia's face right below her eyes, to the left of her nose. The pain was enormous, as if Richard had taken a bat against her skull. Her face went numb as she fell back against the bed. Chris awoke then, confused, stunned. His initial reaction was to think it was a joke being played by one of his brothers, but he saw his wife and the blood that ran down her face. A bullet fired from Richard's gun, shooting through his temple. Chris wondered if it was really the Night Stalker. The force of the bullet knocked him back. And Richard went to shoot Virginia again, laughing crazily.

Their five-year-old daughter woke up, screaming and crying.

Chris was the only barrier left protecting his family from the psychopath who'd broken into his home. At six-foot-one, Chris rose from the ground and attacked the predator. The sudden attack by the strong man shocked Richard. He ran, screaming at Chris to stay back, but Chris was in full protection mode. Richard fired twice, missing both times. They wrestled for a bit. Chris wanted nothing more than to kill the man who'd shot his wife. But Richard was quick and slipped away, running for the sliding glass door. Chris pursued him to the door even with a bullet lodged in the base of his brain. But he stopped there and shouted for help.

Safe in his car, Richard thought to reload his gun and shoot the man who was screaming for help up, but decided it was too much of a risk.

Instead of waiting for the ambulance to arrive, Chris loaded his family and drove them to the hospital, where they were all treated for their wounds.

When the Peterson attack hit the press, reporters were hungry. Frank Salerno decided to enter a dialogue with the killer. He went to the press with a quote. "In this attack, the Stalker showed his true colors." Frank was calling Richard a coward.

And the serial killer took the bait. When he read the morning newspaper with the quote, Richard became enraged.

What he did—breaking into people's homes—he believed took courage. They didn't understand the dangers that he put himself into doing the work of Satan. Richard decided that for his next attack, he would need a bit more firepower. He decided on an Uzi, which he purchased from one of his regular dealers at the bus terminal.

Heavy metal blasted in the stolen car as he drove out east. He'd never been this far in that direction before, and figured the security and fear would be down. The night was dark and Richard was ready; he drove along the upscale streets of Diamond Bar. This time, he'd show the police he was fearless. He stopped in front of the home of Sakina and Elyas Abowath.

Another young couple in their late twenties and early thirties, they had two boys under the age of three. He found the sliding glass door was unlocked, and with deadly silence, he entered the home. Richard Ramirez moved through the halls. He took inventory of all those asleep, first peering into the room of their three-year-old son. He found Sakina and Elyas snoring in their king bed, the crib of their ten-week-old baby close to the edge. Sakina had finally fallen asleep moments before. It was just after 2:30 a.m.

Richard decided that before he committed murder, it would be best to bring his car closer for a quick escape. He hurried out and boldly parked his stolen car right in the home's driveway, as though he owned the house himself.

Returning returned to the place he'd just left, he used the .25 to shoot Elyas in the head, killing him instantly. He lunged over the dying body, jumping onto Sakina, punching her stomach and face. She awoke to a maniac atop of her. Sweat ran down his skin. His eyes were wild and hungry. "Don't scream, bitch, or I'll kill you and your kids here and now!"

She remained silent as he shoved a shirt so far down her throat she began to choke and gag. He bound her ankles together with another shirt and punched her repeatedly, until the world became a daze. Blood dripped from her mouth. She didn't move as Richard began searching through their home, tearing through it all. He began his process of demanding the location of the valuables and beating Sakina into answering him. He dragged her through the house by her hair as if she weighed nothing, tearing away her nightgown. Then he raped her, forcing her to perform oral on him as well as sodomizing her. He went as far to drink some of her breast milk.

Her thoughts raced about her children. She had to do whatever it took to keep them alive and safe. As Richard raped her, excited by the sheer terror he was inflicting upon this family, the three-year-old awoke.

"Shut that kid up!" Richard demanded.

"Please let me go to him; I'll keep him quiet; please don't hurt him."

"Swear on Satan you won't scream."

"I swear on Satan," she vowed. "I swear on Satan I won't scream."

Her hands were still bound tightly as she entered her son's bedroom. Richard was close behind. Naked, bloodied, and bruised, Sakina could only nestle her head beside her child, whispering to him to go back to sleep. He did then, drifting away.

Richard seized ahold of Sakina and threw her back into the bedroom, where he continued to rape her, reveling in his total domination. He beat her over and over, inflicting rounds of terror, performing whatever horror he needed to find the location of the valuables.

After he was finished and the home ransacked, he left Sakina and her three-year-old tied up in the home. He only left after Sakina swore to Satan that she'd revealed all the diamonds and jewels to Richard. He departed with a pillowcase full.

Minutes after the killer disappeared in the dark, Sakina reached out to her son as far as she could. Her hand had been handcuffed to the doorknob. She was able to untie her son's hands, who in turn freed his legs. She told her three year old to go to the neighbor's house. Richard had dismantled the phones. The prospect of venturing out in the dark, late at night, scared Sakina's son, but she assured him the neighbors would have candy and treats waiting. That was enough to bolster his courage, and the three-year-old ran out of the house to find the neighbors, who were more than shocked to find the child ringing the doorbell in the early hours of the morning.

He seemed to be on a mission to obtain ice cream. There was nothing left to do but return him home. There the neighbors came upon the horrific scene. Sakina lay naked and beaten, handcuffed to the door.

The horror continued to spread, and the fear throughout southern California was at an all-time high. While Richard was enjoying the notoriety, he needed to appease Satan elsewhere, where the people felt safe. With so many on edge, his job was rising in challenge.

Sixty-two-year-old Jesse Perez was a small time thief. He hung around the bus terminal in LA and had taken notice of Richard. He worked as a cab driver, had heard the news, and believed the man he knew as Rick was indeed the Night Stalker. The Rick he knew around the bus terminal had bad teeth, smelled like wet leather, and wore all black. There was a large sum of reward money attached to the Night Stalker's identity, and Perez couldn't pass it up. Out of fear, he had his daughter step forward and let the police know she knew who the Night Stalker was.

But Richard was on his way to San Francisco in a stolen Mercedes. He arrived in the late afternoon heat and checked into the Bristol hotel. He spent the day scoring some pot and watching a porno playing in one of the booths at the adult stores. He made his way to Chinatown eventually and shadowed a woman for a bit. He waited until she entered a two-story building, and without hesitation, Richard knocked her down using his bare fists, beating her into a bloody pulp. He was certain Satan would love his raw brutality.

At 2 a.m. on August 18, Richard began his normal hunt. He picked a two-story yellow stucce, belonging to Peter and Barbara Pan, who were both in their early sixties. They slept soundly as Richard entered the home. He shot Peter in the temple with his .25, killing him immediately. Barbara awoke in a panic. Richard beat her, then sexually assaulted her, but when she resisted him, he shot her straight in the head.

Tearing through the home, he stole what he could find, and before leaving he took one of Barbara's lipstick tubes and with it wrote "Jack the Knife" on the wall along with a pentagram beneath in an attempt to throw the police. Richard believed he was smarter than all of them.

The volume of violence left Richard in a state of arousal, pulsing with sexual energy. He stopped and picked up a prostitute to take her back to his hotel and have sex with her feet for ten dollars.

Peter and Barbara's thirty-one-year-old son discovered the bodies of his parents the next morning at 10:30 a.m. With tears and shaking hands, he called the police.

Salerno and Carillo heard the news of the San Francisco attack and knew immediately the Night Stalker had made his way north. They spoke with the heads of the San Francisco Stalker task force and laid out all the facts of the attack along with the LA murders. Both groups agreed to start sharing information about the cases. It would be the only way to stop him. Richard's methods hadn't changed, but it was clear his location had.

The news and information reached the Mayor of San Francisco in no time. Dianne Feinstein held a news conference. She revealed details of the case that were not meant for the public—details that reached the ears of Richard Ramirez. He learned that they knew about his Avia sneakers as well as the ballistic report. He had no idea his shoes were linking him to the murders, and realized it was time to change things up a bit.

Frank Salerno and Gil Carillo were enraged upon seeing the televised news conference. All their hard-earned evidence was being left for the killer to find.

And at 8 p.m., the day of the conference, Richard made his way to the center of the Golden Gate Bridge. The sun was dripping into the horizon, setting shades of orange and red across the sky. Richard tossed his size 11.5 sneakers over the edge and into the water.

August 25 rolled around. Richard had wasted his days smoking pot constantly, listening to heavy metal and watching pornos. But he'd had enough of San Francisco. It was too cramped, far too small for him to disappear into the sea of the unknown. Richard hopped in the stolen Mercedes and decided it was time he returned home to the city of LA.

When he made it back, he rented a room in Chinatown. There he hunkered down and read as much as he could about his murders. All the information delighted him. He was proud that his acts had garnished so much attention, so much fear. But at this high level of fame, Richard knew he'd have to be more careful. He had to stop business with his usual fence. The man knew too much and was a risk

It was time to kill again. Richard swapped out the Mercedes for an orange Toyota and hit the streets, cruising. It was Sunday night, and at 1 a.m., he paid a visit to Mission Viejo.

But his visit would not go unnoticed.

James Romero III, thirteen years old, was in his driveway during the warm late summer night. He was working on his scooter and saw the orange Toyota drive slowly down the street without its lights on. He took note of the driver and the car. He didn't recognize it as one of his neighbors. Something about it all seemed off. He thought of writing down the license plate, but didn't. Richard didn't see the boy watching. Instead, his focus was on the next house to ransack and inflict a wave of terror on in the name of Satan.

He picked out the home of twenty-nine-year-old Bill Carns, who was living with his twenty-seven-year-old fiancée, Carole Smith.

The sound of the metal automatic being cocked jerked Bill from his sleep. The Night Stalker had come to their home. Both had been reading the news and had spoken earlier that evening about purchasing a gun or bars for the window. Bill downplayed his wife's fear. Nothing had happened in Mission Viejo.

Bill leaped out of bed, moving fast. Richard shot him in the head. The force of the bullet knocked him backward. Richard stepped forward, moving in, and fired the gun two more times. Out of the corner of his eye he saw movement from beneath the covers of the bed and ripped them off to find a horrified Carole.

"Shut up, bitch, or I'll blow your head off," he growled. Her mouth stayed tightly sealed.

By a fistful of hair, Richard ripped her from the bed and threw her to the floor. He used ties from the closet to hog tie Carole, all the while beating and punching her. When she cried out, he demanded she swear her love to Satan. Through tears and a shaking voice, she pledged her love. He slapped and kicked her, demanding to know the location of the valuables.

He returned to the bed. Carole was stricken with fear. She could not move, as Richard unzipped his pants, telling her to lie on her back. He forced her legs apart and assaulted her. The stench of his breath only made the matters more sickening.

It didn't take him long to search through the home. He was an expert now, and knowing where jewels and money were kept was second nature. He blew through the home. She showed him the money stashed away in the dresser. He pocketed the $400. Turning to face Carole, he said, "You know, this is all that saved you. This is all your life is worth. I would have killed you if it weren't for this money." When he stopped looking, he forced Carole to swear to Satan there was nothing left. She swore.

He pushed her down to her knees and brutally forced her to orally copulate him.

When he was finished, much to her surprise, Richard met her lips with his own and kissed her tenderly. Richard left her then. He exited the house and slipped into the orange Toyota, making his return trip to Chinatown.

But thirteen-year-old Romero was still outside in the driveway. He saw what he described as "the weird-looking guy in black" a second time. And this time, he was sure to get the plate number. He ran inside to tell his parents. They phoned the police.

Sweat dripped off Richard's skin. The air was suffocating, and with the gloves on, his hands became dry. Richard couldn't take it anymore, and he removed his gloves while driving. He would have to be extra sure when he wiped the car down for prints not to leave anything behind. So when he dumped the car in a small shopping mall, he used a cloth to go over the steering wheel and anywhere else he might have touched with his bare hands.

Except Richard missed one spot. He'd left a print on the rear view mirror.

He slept soundly that night after taking a bus back to Chinatown, completely oblivious to the clues that would undermine his reign as the servant for the Prince of Darkness.

Drifter from El Paso

Jesse Perez's daughter contacted the sheriff's office on August 27th to inform them about the man her father knew from the bus terminal. She wanted to ensure her father would not get tangled up in any trouble after going to the police. He himself had a bit of a record. They were ensured nothing would happen, and so Jesse Perez came forward with the name of the Night Stalker: Rick.

He told the police how he first came to meet Richard along with his older brother, who both hung around the bus terminal. Jesse even purchased a .22 automatic from Rick. He described the man as an avid burglar who came from El Paso and had bad teeth, as related in the newspaper. One evening, Rick had even gone so far as to tell Perez about an Asian couple he'd killed. Perez told Frank and Gil, "He's a loner and always talkin' 'bout how great Satan is. I don't believe in none of that shit, but he for sure and for real does. He likes that heavy metal music. Always has a Walkman."

He let them know about the arrest of Richard last December, when the man drove a stolen car into the bus terminal while jacked up on cocaine. If they could pull that arrest record, they'd have his info.

Perez also left with the detectives one last vital piece of information. He told them about Rick's fence, Felipe Solano. "He's got all kinds of shit in there—televisions, radios, VCRs, jewelry ... a ton of shit, man, all the way up to the fucking ceiling ... he's Rick's fence," Perez told them. He didn't lie. Inside Solano's, police found a vat of evidence. Almost all the stolen items from the murders were stockpiled away in the fence's home. Felipe Solano swore he didn't have Richard's full name, address, or phone.

The police began to dig through records, searching for the arrest that matched Richard's accident in December 1984.

In San Francisco, the police were busy at work as well. They decided to put an ad in the newspaper asking if anyone had purchased the stolen jewelry from the Pans murder. They knew someone had to be buying the goods. They released detailed descriptions and photos, hoping for a match.

One turned up—Donna Meyers. Donna had bought the jewelry from Richard. She'd given the Pans' golden bracelet and several pieces to her daughter-in-law. They recognized the jewelry right away and spoke with the police. Richard was an acquaintance of Donna's. She'd met him on several occasions and knew him to be a professional thief who loved AC/DC and Satan, and had terrible teeth. Donna had met him through a friend. She directed the authorities to Armando Rodriguez, whom she'd lived with and in 1979 had visited El Paso. There, she'd met Richard for the first time.

With a close acquaintance at hand, the police made their way to Armando Rodriguez, who at first put up a fight. The police warned him that withholding information would make him an accomplice to the Night Stalker. Armando wanted nothing to do with the murders and finally gave them a full name. Richard Ramirez.

Hundreds of files came up with that same name, but the police were not just one step closer. They were miles ahead.

After the orange Toyota was located, thanks to the wise and observant thirteen-year-old, a print was pulled from the rear view mirror. The print was compared to all the Richard Ramirezes on file. Finally, a tall, thin, small-time thief drifter from El Paso came up. They had a face and a name.

And in the morning, Richard Ramirez landed a spot on every newspaper and news station. The dark, penetrating gaze and matted black hair of Richard's mugshot was the front cover of the media.

But he was completely unaware.

Saturday morning, Richard left the bus terminal. The police scoured the area, hungrily looking for their killer. Frank Salerno had spent the night prior driving the streets late at night, hoping to run into Richard.

But Richard had been away visiting his family and was now on the returning bus to LA. He'd spent time with Robert and his wife Samantha. They'd had a daughter who was now two years old and were living out in Tucson, Arizona.

He hopped off the bus and made his way through, passing by the police without raising an eyebrow. It wasn't until he stood at the counter at the liquor store that he was spotted by the elderly women behind him. It was then that Richard saw his face on the cover of the magazine, sitting on the counter. He grabbed the magazine and ran.

Before he'd gotten far, the store owner had already contacted the police. The cruisers were dispatched, and helicopters took to the sky. The chase was on. The sharp sound of sirens sang around Richard as his legs pedaled him forward. His eyes darted through the news article as he read. They'd found him after all.

He vaulted himself over a six-foot fence. Running, he knew the last thing he could do was stop. He ditched his black pack in the yard and continued to sprint. His lungs screamed and his muscles grew fatigued. He made it the highway, where cars whipped past. Then he darted across the busy freeway and bolted up a hill, jumped over yet another fence, and hopped onto the first bus he saw.

Richard was drenched in so much sweat that it looked like a bucket of water had been dumped on him. He paid the bus fare and took a seat. His heart pounded. Right away, the passengers recognized Richard, pointing. The bus stopped, and he got off. There was nowhere for Richard to hide. Everyone, it seemed, knew his face.

If Richard wanted a chance to survive, he would need a car.

Police zoomed helicopters overhead, searching the area. A lone woman sat in the passenger seat of a running car on the corner of the street. Her boyfriend had darted inside the grocery shop to grab a few things and she was waiting when she noticed a deranged man staring at her, coming toward her.

Richard attempted to grapple the woman out of the car, but she put up a fight, immediately shouting for help. Her boyfriend and another man came running out. They recognized Richard as the Night Stalker.

It was a failed carjackng, and Richard had no choice but to rely on his legs. He took off then, bolting forward. But he was pursued. He raced now. The air whizzed past his ears as he clamored up fences, jumping into yards. But he couldn't escape. The neighborhood came to life and the home owners chased him down. One man beat him with a spatula he'd been using while grilling when Richard landed in his backyard. The streets filled with shouts as the neighbors called out "El Matador!"

Richard finally made the mistake of attempting to jack Manuel De La Torre's car from the driveway. Manuel heard the cries of his wife, saw the tears running down her face and knew immediately. He grabbed a metal bar, and outside he found the Night Stalker trying desperately to start his car. Manuel opened the car door and cracked Richard hard on the head with the rod. Richard jumped out and began to run, but Manuel and several others were right behind him. They watched as Richard turned, sticking his tongue out at his pursuers and hissing like a snake.

Within reach, Manuel swung. The metal bar came crashing down on Richard's skull. He fell hard onto the pavement.

The LAPD and LASD finally arrived on the scene and the police officers realized that the man lying on the pavement, beaten by the LA residents, was none other than the Night Stalker.

With a throbbing head and intense pain, Richard was handcuffed and taken away. "Why don't you just shoot me? I deserve to die. Now they're going to send me to the electric chair. I was being chased all the way from Olympic, you know. All the killings are going to be blamed on me. You see, those people wanted to kill me," Richard rambled to the officers.

At the station, Richard was for the most part quiet. They brought him into a room for questioning and sat him down, making sure he was secured. At one point, Richard began to slam his head against the table, humming AC/DC's "Night Prowler."

He asked the sergeant across from him what day it was. Then Richard said, "I want the electric chair. They should have shot me on the street. I did it, you know. You guys got me—the Night Stalker … hey, let me have a gun to play Russian roulette. I'd rather die than spend the rest of my life in prison. Can you imagine? The people caught me, not the police." A laugh broke from his throat as he continued, "You think I'm crazy, but you don't know Satan. Of course I did it, so what? Give me your gun, I'll take care of myself. You know I'm a killer, so shoot me. I deserve to die. You can see Satan on my arm."

The news broke out that the Night Stalker had been captured. Word reached his family, who couldn't believe it. At first they prayed that this was some twisted lie. Their Richard was incapable of such things.

"Haven't I been a good father?" Julian Ramirez asked his son Joseph. "I always worked; I always sacrificed; I did everything I could. What did I do to deserve such a thing?"

"It's a mistake, Richie didn't kill all those people. No way. He stole things, yeah, but he's no killer. No way. It's a mistake, Dad."

"I hope so. Marijuana. It's all because he smoked marijuana," Julian insisted. He drank that night, something Julian rarely did. Then he went to his bedroom drawer and took out a gun, telling Joseph he could not bear the disgrace his son brought upon the family. He would kill himself and then Mercedes. Joseph fought his father and took the gun. He locked it away in the trunk of his car. Julian cried himself to sleep, and Ruth gave her mother sleeping pills. The reporters called and swarmed the house the following days. When one asked Julian about Richard, he simply responded, "In my heart I cannot believe he would have arrived at that! But if the authorities have proof, what can we do?"

Trial of Satan's Servant

By the time the trial arrived, the State of California had already spent $1,301,836 on Richard Ramirez. The preliminary hearings had dragged on as well as the juror selection. And on January 10, 1989, Richard had his first day of trial. He hadn't done well in prison. He'd put on weight, about twenty pounds, and his miserable behavior was even more evident in the courtroom.

Throughout the process, he hired and fired many lawyers for whatever reason he deemed fit at the moment. He often called the judge a motherfucker and wore thick, giant sunglasses to sleep behind. He snarled at the press and reporters, but sought out the women in court, often making flirtatious gestures and faces toward them.

Fan mail from these admirers poured into Richard's cell. Women lined up to visit Richard and have their moment with the killer. Some even smuggled in phallic vegetables to the visitation booth so he might watch them pleasure themselves with them. Or they'd lift their skirts so he could catch a view of their privates. One woman told

Richard that after court one day, the description of one of his murders sexually excited her.

Another woman wrote to him, describing her fantasy of having sex with Richard in a cemetery, a top of an overturned tombstone, and he would be covered in the blood of one of his victims. He also was told about a fantasy involving him and a woman making love in a coffin. It would be their love nest.

True crime author Doreen Lioy was completely infatuated with Richard, to the point of obsession. To her, all of Richard's other fans were nothing more than a "bunch of street sluts." On weekends, she would come at 5 a.m. to ensure a spot in the front of line to see Richard. She would stand and wait in the dark morning. She wanted to marry him and have children with him, making sure that whatever he wanted in jail, she found a way to bring to him, including books or money. When asked about the trial and murders, she claimed, "None of that matters. I love him for who he is. You have to take the good with the bad when you're in love." She later would say, "I'd cut off my right arm for him." The two eventually married while Richard was serving his time. He loved that she was still a virgin. She was completely his. Not like the other women.

Doreen went to every day of trial.

And as it continued, Richard saw it as nothing more than a farce to him. He pleaded not guilty. He may have done so just to listen to his victims come to court and retell their terrifying experiences with Richard. There they would sit and face their attacker and recount. Richard at times would look bored, amused, and even aroused. Though when his father stepped up to testify, Richard struggled to look at him.

Pasadena Star-News editor Frank Girardot covered the trial. He later recounted it. "It was televised," he said. "It lasted several weeks—I think it went from July until September. It involved a lot of gruesome testimony and a lot of theatrics from the defendant. He would draw pentagrams on his hand and hold it up for the cameras. He would smile at people. At one point, a juror was killed—turns out it was by her boyfriend—but it was certainly a scary time."

Once, the judge asked Richard to remove a hat in the courtroom. He screamed, "No!" like a spoiled child. He referred to the press as a bunch of grubby parasites.

In his cell, Richard masturbated constantly, like a caged animal in heat. Full of need, restless. He decorated it with photographs of his murders, including one of Maxine Zazzara, and because they were evidence for the trial and defense, the police could not take them down. He fought with the prisoners and harassed the bailiffs. His words were aggressive and spiteful.

After his arrest, Richard had spent four-and-half-years in court. At 2:12 p.m. on September 20, 1989, everyone gathered in the courtroom to hear the jury's verdict. Frank Salerno and Gil Carillo's tireless work finally paid off. Richard was found guilty for every single charge of the forty-six. He listened in his holding cell. His composure was calm and he was described as stoic.

For the Ramirez family, they continued to struggle with the truth of who their son was. Julian told a reporter from the *El Paso Herald Post* that if his son was guilty, then he deserved the punishment, but added, "I don't know if he did it or not. But if he did, he didn't do it by himself. Why don't the police investigate to see who else was involved? I've accepted he was a thief, but I've never accepted that he did the things they say he did. The media turned him into a monster. He's really just a poor boy who was raised to believe in God."

The penalty phase came next, but Richard told his lawyers he had no desire to fight. When they told Richard bluntly that if he didn't put up a fight he would certainly face the death penalty, Richard simply said, "Well, then let them. Fuck them. Dying doesn't scare me. I'll be in hell. With Satan. That's gotta be a better place than this. I'd rather die than live in a cage. Fuck that shit, man,"

He received the death penalty via lethal injection. When the sentence was given, Richard asked to be heard. In the courtroom surrounded by news reporters and cameras, Richard unfolded a piece of a paper and began to read aloud.

"You don't understand me. You are not expected to. You are not capable. I am beyond your experience. I am beyond good and evil. I will be avenged. Lucifer dwells in all of us. I don't know why I'm even wasting my breath, but what the hell. For what is said of my life, there have been lies in the past and there will be lies in the future. I don't believe in the hypocritical, moralistic dogma of this so-called civilized society. I need not look beyond this courtroom to see all the liars, the haters, the killers, the crooks, the paranoid cowards. Truly the *Trematodes* of the earth. You maggots make me sick! Hypocrites one and all. We are all expendable for a cause. No one knows that better than those who kill for policy, clandestinely or openly, as do the governments of the world, which kill in the name of God and country ... I don't need to hear all of society's rationalizations. I've heard them all before ... legions of the night, night breed, repeat not the errors of the night prowler and show no mercy."

He was given the death sentence nineteen times.

Afterward, he famously said, "Big deal. Death always went with the territory." Then he played on a Ramirez family inside joke: "See you in Disneyland."

But Richard never received the sentence given to him. His days dragged on in prison. He spent time reading the mail that came in, and seeing his wife, Doreen, on the weekend visits. He hated being locked up and never feared the death sentence, but over the years, he grew accustomed to the lifestyle. Though, there was no rush made for his appeal. The longer the wait, the more time Richard had alive.

Before his death, he was asked how a person could avoid being caught by a serial killer. He responded, "You can't. Once they are focused on you, have you where you are vulnerable, you're all theirs. Dahmer used to invite you home for a drink, and the next thing you knew, he's eating you. Same thing with John Gacy: he'd put on his clown face, do a couple of tricks, and suddenly he had you handcuffed and in his control. What people can do is not trust someone you don't know and to always be aware of what's going on around you. When you drop your guard—that's when a serial killer moves."

After almost a quarter-century on death row, Richard Ramirez became ill. He was taken from death row to the hospital on a Thursday. His skin was a bright green color. He displayed signs of severe jaundice in his last moments.

Frank Salerno had made a promise to come to Richard's execution, but the promise would never be fulfilled. On June 7, 2013, Richard drew his last breath after a battle with lymphoma and liver failure. He suffered from hepatitis C, which is spread from use of intravenous drugs. He was fifty-three.

The Night Stalker's reign had ended.

"The death of Richard Ramirez in prison today closes a dark chapter in the history of Los Angeles," LAPD Chief Charlie Beck said upon his death. "Let's not forget the victims who suffered at his hands and the victims' families who are still suffering with the memories of their lost loved ones."

Printed in Great Britain
by Amazon

55776383R00099